Clutter Coach
Success Secrets

Strategies, Inspiration,
and Motivation to
Create a Clutter-Free Life

Kathi J. Miller

Clutter Coach Success Secrets

Strategies, Inspiration,
and Motivation to
Create a Clutter-Free Life

Kathi J. Miller

Printed by Create Space, an Amazon.com Company.

ISBN-13: 978-1540626509
ISBN-10: 1540626504

Dedicated to my husband, Steve
who ensures I practice what I preach!!

Table of Contents

Month-by-Month Action Plan

Stories

Change Your Mind

Change Your Behavior

Final Words

Introduction

In November of 2005, I decided to begin a monthly newsletter, the Clutter Coach Success Secrets, for my clients and the people who attended my speeches and classes. I knew many of them shared similar clutter challenges.

I wanted to inspire and motivate them to keep working on their clutter. And I was frustrated with the endless flow of publicity on the use of bins and baskets which just create more stuff!

I wanted to provide real solutions that anyone could implement. Solutions that would lead to life-long habits that create and maintain a clutter-free life.

People with clutter are often perfectionists and procrastinators. Hence, the numerous admonitions to bypass perfectionism and prompts to take immediate action!

I started with a small list of a few hundred of my program attendees. I figured that I had enough material and ideas to write once a month for at least two years. After that, I would re-evaluate to see if I wanted to continue the newsletter. Thousands of subscribers and 11 years later, it's still going strong!

This book is a compilation of my best insight into the causes of clutter and my most practical advice on how to deal with it.

It's divided into five sections.

The first is a month-by-month journey through one year. Start in the current month and do the exercises for each month. A year from now, you'll have less clutter and the skills to maintain a clutter-free life.

The second section is two short stories I wrote about two co-workers from different backgrounds and their approaches to work-related events.

The third and fourth sections are newsletters that represent the two ways to deal with clutter: change your mind about your belongings and change your behavior with respect to your belongings.

The final section is a tribute to my mother who is largely responsible for my clutter-free life habits and attitudes.

Start anywhere in the book. Start in the area of your life that's easiest for you and work up to the more challenging stuff. The most important part is that you BEGIN. Start now!

Month-by-Month Action Plan

Fling It Today!
January 2015

As I read the newspaper feature describing all the ways to re-purpose your 2014 calendar I screamed to myself "No, No, Noooooooo!!" Do you need more framed stuff on your walls, more greeting cards, more vases, more gift tags, more to do? I sure don't, and I bet you don't either.

This month is the first installment in a series, using the word "FIT" as an acronym for a type of de-cluttering. Each monthly segment is designed to help you move through this year - lighter, happier, with less stress and more satisfaction in your life.

January FIT = Fling It Today! We'll start off the year with the easy stuff. Things you can get rid of without agonizing decision-making or emotional wrangling. It's rapid weight-loss for your home!

Step One: Pack away your perfectionism. See your perfectionism as a skill that is useful and sometimes essential in the workplace, but it will get in the way of your decluttering, so pack it away for today.

Use 3 containers - Garbage, Recycling, Donation - not the perfect ones, whatever is handy!

Start in your bathroom.

Garbage:Throw out the slivers of soap. (Remember perfectionism is packed away!) Make-up can breed bacteria. Get rid of make-up that is old or rarely used.

Recycle: Gather up all the body wash and shampoo containers with a small amount left. Tell the truth - how long have they been in your shower? Rinse them out and recycle the containers.

Donate: Any toiletries, make-up, and over the counter medications that are unopened can be donated to your local Women's shelter.

Did you get some bath products for Christmas that you know you won't use? How about the free samples that came with a cosmetic purchase that aren't your colors? Or the multiple bottles of shampoo you bought right before you switched brands? Let this stuff go and have room in your bathroom cabinets!

The kitchen is your next stop.

Garbage: We're looking for items to quickly toss, so start with the spices. If they're expired, really old, no longer appropriately scented, discolored or faded, out they go. By the way, dried basil is supposed to be green not gray!

Recycle: Where have you been stashing your grocery bags? In the front hall closet? By the back stairs? Wherever they are hiding, drag them all out and recycle all but the few you might use in the near future. Assign a small spot for them to live so they don't get out of hand again. Paper bags can go right in the recycling bin. Every grocery store and many other stores have a container inside their entrance for plastic bags. Create some bags of plastic bags and put them in your car.

Donate: Unexpired food that you know you won't use. Maybe you bought cans of pumpkin when they were on sale in early November, but ended up serving a store-bought pumpkin pie for Thanksgiving. How about the ingredients for the fancy holiday cookies you never got around to making? Did you buy special food for visiting relatives that is edible and unopened, but your family won't eat it? Take these to your local grocer and put them in the bin for the food pantry.

Now consider your holiday "leftovers."

Garbage: If there's an ornament or decor item waiting to be repaired, perhaps it's been on your kitchen island since last year, throw it out today. If you've assigned some special meaning to this inanimate object take a picture of it and then throw it away. These items are not designed to last forever. Is there a string of lights that won't light up anymore? Set your timer for one minute. If you can't find the misbehaving bulb in that time frame, throw out the lights.

Recycle: Holiday cards. You don't have to record who sent you cards and to whom you sent cards. Lots of people stopped doing this or never did it and they are perfectly happy! Just take the entire set of cards and put them into the recycling bin. If you have cards from previous years, go grab those and do the same. Breathe a deep sigh of relief!! Catalogs - you have enough stuff, you can stop shopping now. Put the catalogs into the recycling bin and walk away quickly.

Donate: Are there holiday decorations you don't use anymore? You don't need to wait until next year, donate them today. Any presents that just don't work for you that you can't return? Donate them, too. "The person is not the thing and the thing is not the person." Getting rid of a gift does not negate your relationship with the gift giver.

Super Quick and Easy!

Take the pretty shopping bags you've kept but don't use and give one to each family member. Set a timer for 15 minutes and challenge each person to fill up their bag with items to donate. There is only one rule - it must be something that belongs to that person; they can't get rid of anyone else's stuff. Books, games, DVDs, clothes, shoes, whatever is no longer being used is fair game. Take the items to your favorite charity. Then go have some fun together with the people you love.

My Mother's Motto: "People less fortunate can use what we're not using."

Happy FIT New Year!!

Five Items Today
February 2015

Clutter-free living is a skill, and like all skills it requires practice. This month I challenge you to practice clutter-free living by getting rid of 5 items every day.

I've made it as easy as possible. I chose the shortest month and I'm providing a daily suggestion. If you skip a day or more, don't try to catch up, just do the 5 items for the current date. Repeat the process for as many days as possible. If a daily item doesn't apply to you, choose one on your own or repeat one from another day.

Donate or toss items as needed.

If you do this exercise, three things can happen. One, by March first, you'll have 140 fewer belongings. Two, on any day you may decide to get rid of more - always an option. Three, you'll be acquiring a skill you can apply for the rest of your life!

FEBRUARY

1 - While you're preparing for the Super Bowl, get rid of 5 mugs.

2 - Ground Hog Day! Today get rid of 5 dried up pens or markers.

3 - 5 old emails (or 50!)

4 - 5 magazines or catalogs

5 - 5 pairs of socks with holes or 5 pairs of socks you don't wear

6 - 5 stained plastic containers or 5 good containers you don't use

7 - It's the weekend! Toss 5 old photos or photo albums

8 - Go through the games or puzzles today and get rid of at least 5.

9 - It's Monday, grab 5 empty boxes on your way out the door!

10 - 5 empty jars or bottles

11 - 5 gadgets you don't use

12 - 5 rags

13 - Friday, the 13th! Be brave! Get rid of 5 cookbooks or recipes.

14 - It's Valentine's Day! Donate 5 florist vases.

15 - 5 dead, dried up, or artificial plants.

16 - 5 tools or pieces of hardware. How many nails will you use?

17 - It's Mardi Gras! Celebrate by getting rid of 5 pieces of jewelry.

18 - 5 sets of mailing labels or greeting cards sent by charities.

19 - 5 decor items: picture frames or knick knacks

20 - 5 tote bags or shopping bags

21 - Get the family involved today. Donate 5 coats or jackets.

22 - Donate 5 pairs of gloves/mittens or 5 scarves.

23 - 5 CDs, DVDs, or Video Tapes

24 - 5 kitchen appliances you don't use: Bread machine?

25 - 5 old towels. Donate to the Humane Society.

26 - 5 items of spoiled food in the fridge

27 - 5 pairs of uncomfortable shoes

28 - 5 Regrets or Resentments. Let them go.

Focus on what you've accomplished this month instead!

30 Day Challenge
March 2016

Thirty-Day challenges are common, especially when it comes to fitness. They often feature activities that take a few minutes per day such as push-ups, planks, or toe touches. They're popular because people can make a short-term commitment and see results.

The concept of the 30-day challenge lends itself perfectly to decluttering. For this month's challenge, you have 3 options. Choose any one and do it for the entire month. You'll see results and you'll feel freer by April.

Option 1. If you have piles of papers you need to wade through for your taxes, set a timer for 5 minutes every day and tackle a small pile. At the end of the month, you'll have spent a total of 2.5 hours on this project. It's tempting to think that the "perfect way" is to spend 2.5 hours in one chunk, but that's not practical for most people. You can accomplish as much or more in regular, focussed bursts of energy. Try it!!

Option 2: Walk 10 minutes a day at 3 miles per hour, and you'll walk 15 miles this month! If you walk 4 miles per hour, you'll log 20 miles. What does this have to do with decluttering? Fresh air is great for mental decluttering. And exercise energizes you to declutter your dwelling. If you already exercise regularly, add 5 or 10 minutes per day.

Option 3. Get rid of one accessory or piece of jewelry every day this month.

Plan ahead. Schedule your daily challenge. If possible, choose the same time each day. When you wake up in the morning, know when you'll be doing the challenge. Don't wait until the end of the day when you're too tired.

For each choice, the daily practice is key to developing new habits. If you're inclined to tell yourself that you need large blocks of time to accomplish decluttering, the daily doses will help convince you otherwise.

That's it! Choose one and begin!

Spring Clean Your Schedule
April 2016

Spring is a great time to clean out the old and make way for the new. This month I recommend Spring Cleaning your schedule. Take a good look at how you are spending your time and make adjustments as needed.

ROI or Return on Investment is usually used to describe the rate of return on the investment of money in a financial transaction. We already use some of the same terms to describe our use of money and time such as wasting money/wasting time and spending money/spending time. I like to apply the concept of ROI on the investment of my time. What do I get out of spending my time in a certain way? For example, daily exercise provides a positive return on the investment of my time, as does taking the time to shop for and prepare healthy food. I invest my time in getting enough sleep, engaging in creative pursuits, and spending time with friends who uplift me.

How are you spending your valuable time each day? And what's the return on your investment of that time? For example, when you get home from work, do you plunk yourself down in front of the TV? Do you feel energized after doing so? Would you get a better return on your investment of time by walking outside? You don't have to like doing it, you can just like the result of having done it!

How much time do you spend on Social Media? Ten or fifteen years ago we were not engaged in this manner, so what's the return you've gotten on your investment of possibly huge chunks of your time on Facebook, Twitter, Instagram, Pinterest, LinkedIn, Google+, etc? You may respond that it helps you keep in touch with others, which might be the case. However, before your interaction with these sites, did you even care what some of these people you now follow were doing in their daily lives? Tell the truth.

If you're one of the millions of people who pay money each month to follow the lives of certain entertainers, are you getting a good Return On Investment of your money, or would that money be better spent saving for a vacation?

Clutter-free living requires you to take an honest look at your time, energy, and financial resources and make conscious decisions that serve you. If you're paying attention to what everyone else is eating, drinking, wearing, watching, listening to, reading, thinking, and doing, how much time do you have for your own life?

You deserve to live a clutter-free life.
Begin Today!

PLAN = Prepare List As Needed
May 2008

Suppose I told you that by spending 30 minutes on one specific activity you could save hundreds of dollars and countless hours of time, would you do it? If I could guarantee it would also save you energy, then would you do it?

It seems simple doesn't it? Save money, time, and energy. Who wouldn't say yes to that? Yet, it has been my experience that people avoid planning like it's a contagious disease.

Yes, 30 minutes of planning right now can save you money, time, and energy for the rest of spring and summer! Here's how. Take out all of your warm weather clothes and put them on your bed. Try them on and only keep the ones that fit. Now, see what outfits you can put together for your real-life activities. You notice I said real-life, not your fantasy life! Be honest about the clothes you will actually wear. You can include jewelry and other accessories, too.

You will quickly see which tops go with which bottoms and where you have gaps in your wardrobe. Take a sheet of paper and a pen. Create your list to be as specific as possible. Wait a few days and check your list. Which items are must-have and which aren't really essential? Shopping uses your precious time and energy even when you don't buy anything. So shop smarter, not longer.

Keep the list handy for shopping in stores and on-line. Remember, just look for the items on your list. This saves lots of time because you are no longer looking at everything that's available, just the items you need. You save money because you're not tempted to buy whatever is a "good deal." It's not a good deal if you don't even need it it at all! Overall you begin to spend less because you see that you only need a few key items. Getting dressed every morning is quicker and easier because you have all the components needed for complete outfits and everything fits!

Once you have what you need, stay out of the stores! Go to the beach, the park, the outdoor concert, whatever you enjoy!

This is also a useful exercise to do with your children. Have a meaningful discussion about how many clothes they <u>need</u> for summer. Teaching them to shop with a list minimizes impulse purchases and in-store arguments about what they want vs. what they need. Stick to the list you create together. Before packing away winter clothes, donate the ones you didn't wear this past winter and those that your kids have outgrown.

What does "enough" mean to you? Consider how many articles of clothing you really need. Are 5 pairs of jeans enough? How about shoes? How many pairs of sandals will you wear during our brief summer? More is not better, it's just more. When you think you need more, you will spend money, time and energy to acquire, maintain and store more. You will have more, but you will not be more satisfied, or more happy, or more creative, or more productive, or more healthy.

Another way to use the PLAN method is in your yard. More pots of flowers are not necessarily better, especially if you buy more than you can take care of. A few well-planned spots of color may be all you need.

Each year, I make notes at the end of summer about the pots of flowers I have on our porch and deck. I have a file called "garden" where I record information about which plants did well in each location and which plants to stop buying because they just don't grow in our yard! If a pot looks especially nice, I'll take a picture of it to remind me the following spring.

My husband grows herbs in several places in our yard. He has photos of the layout of the herb beds so we can watch for signs of herbs regenerating in spring. He also keeps the list of annual herbs we bought the previous year, with notes about how many we'll need the next year.

A small amount of time spent planning in spring and fall saves us time, money, and energy every year. We know exactly how many plants to buy to beautify our home and to enliven our food from May through October!

PLAN = Prepare List as Needed and enjoy the results for months to come!

Four Items Today!
June 2015

It's summer, so there are only four items per day! This month's list features items used frequently in summer or things that might encourage you to clean out your basement or garage. Start by pulling 4 weeds from your garden or from the cracks in your sidewalk.

If you skip a day or more, don't try to catch up, just do the 4 items for the current date and see if you can repeat the process for as many days as possible. If a daily item doesn't apply to you, choose one from the Bonus List below or repeat one from another day. Donate or toss items as needed.

JUNE

1 weeds
2 yard decor - Keep only what you love and use.
3 candles
4 bug spray - How many cans are almost empty?
5 T shirts - How many are ratty looking?
6 caulk, spackle, putty, etc.

7   golf shirts - How many can you wear?

8   sprinklers - Get rid of the broken ones!

9   pajamas - Keep the nice ones!

10 lawn chairs - No, you won't repair these!

11 umbrellas

12 coolers

13 paint rollers & paint supplies

14 chunks of hose and rope - Someday is not a day of the week!

15 water bottles

16 plant pots

17 balls and frisbees - Do you use these anymore?

18 rackets and nets

19 paint & solvents - Start a box for hazardous waste.

20 yard chemicals - More hazardous waste.

21 bikes & bike gear

22 grills and old grill utensils

23 garden tools - How many rakes, trowels & shovels do you use?

24 paper plates - Donate the ones you don't use.

25 underwear - Throw out the ones with holes!

26 sunscreen - Active ingredients degrade within one year of opening, regardless of expiration date.

27 sneakers - or any summer clothing you don't wear or love.

28 freezer contents - How old is this food??

29 swimsuits

30 straws & toothpicks

Bonus List: yard lights, boat supplies, carpet scraps, fishing gear, sandals, camping gear, wood scraps, plastic ware, garden & work gloves, bungee cords, sports equipment.

Happy Clutter-free Summer!

Four Inspiring Tales
July 2015

Four cross country trips to a wedding begin.

Lisa and Jennifer are sisters who pick up their mother in their hometown. They re-connect with friends and relatives and do some genealogical research at the local cemetery before heading out on Route 66 for a leisurely trip.

Samantha is an art teacher with the summer off. She sees this as an opportunity to visit art museums and sculpture gardens. She creates a loose itinerary, tosses some clothes into a suitcase and departs with plenty of time to pursue side-trips at whim.

Newlyweds Alex and Chris take the opposite approach. After securing vacation leave from their respective jobs, they plan out the entire trip and make all the needed reservations. They'll visit major historical sites and friends from college.

Joe is a single parent with 3 teenage sons. He decides that this is the year to finally take his boys on that camping trip he's been promising for years. They research and discuss what to see and where to stay. The process brings them closer together. As the day approaches, they are excited to begin.

These trips are similar to decluttering. Everyone will have a different approach and each one is fine. As long as you stay the course, you'll end up where you're headed. Lisa and Jennifer take a significant trip down Memory Lane, re-living their past. Samantha has some guideposts but is open to changes in plans. Alex and Chris are highly organized and focused on the process as well as the result. Joe may need to give up the belongings from his past so he can be fully present and be an adult role model for his sons.

Each person knows where they're going and how they'll get there. They can't just talk about it, dream about it, plan for it, or buy the gear for it. Their journeys don't begin until they drive away in their vehicles.

No amount of talking about it, reading organizing books, buying bins and baskets, or watching TV shows about it will get you one step closer to a clutter-free life. Decluttering doesn't begin until you've filled a bag or box with recycling, garbage, or donations. There's just no substitute for action!

Schedule appointments with yourself to declutter and keep those appointments. Start today!

Finish It or Let It Go
August 2014

One of the definitions of clutter is "anything unfinished." When you think of something you haven't finished, what comes to mind? Is it the book a friend lent you that you never started? A craft project you purchased months ago, still in its shopping bag? How about that towel bar that needs to be tightened or relocated? Or the super-duper vehicle cleaning you keep promising yourself you'll do?

See these unfinished tasks or projects as open loops. Having too many open loops in your life will trip you up. They'll prevent you from moving forward or at the very least keep from enjoying any fun activities you attempt. They're terrible nags that need to be silenced once and for all.

First, tell the truth about the unfinished business. If you're not going to read the book, give it back. If your enthusiasm for the craft project has waned, donate it. If you don't know how to tighten the towel rack, ask a friend to do it for you. If your car is messy, maybe you need to set new standards of behavior for yourself and your passengers. By the way, entire generations of children grew up NEVER eating or drinking in a car!

Second, decide how to avoid this open loop in the future. Say thanks, but no thanks when someone tries to get you to do something you know you won't do, such as read a book that doesn't interest you. Don't shop at the craft store until and unless you know when you'll make the project. Decide ahead of time if you have the expertise or time to gain such knowledge before you attempt household projects. Not everyone is handy with tools. Keep a garbage bag in your vehicle and empty it daily.

Third, schedule the completion of your current open loops. If you have many of them, choose one. Finish it, then tackle the next one. Resist the perfectionist tendency to think you need days with no interruptions to even begin. That's a fantasy. Most people never have entire days to themselves unless they're sick in bed. All projects can be broken down into tasks. Schedule each small step until it's done. And most importantly, enjoy the results!!

How many projects can you complete or let go of this month?

A clutter-free life is a gift you give yourself and everyone who has to put up with you.

Take Control
September 2008

Do you like to be told what to do? Do you like others controlling you? Most people would answer with a resounding "No" but I maintain that you have allowed yourself to be controlled in many areas of your life. By realizing where and when this is occurring, you can make new choices based on your personal needs, not on what others have decided for you.

When you eat in a restaurant or get fast food at the drive-through, do you eat everything? If so, you have allowed someone else to choose your portion size. If you are older than 25 you may even remember when there were single hamburgers, small fries and 8-ounce drinks!

When you shop for paper towels and buy the multi-packs, you have allowed someone else to determine how many rolls of paper towels you will be storing at home. If you do any shopping without a list, you are at the mercy of the merchandising that has been carefully planned to influence your buying decisions. Food that is at eye level, clothes that are prominently displayed, and sale signs or "bargain aisles" are all designed to get you to make impulse purchases. If you stop for one moment and realize that someone else, some stranger is trying to decide for you what you should buy, then you can see the traps that are set for you whenever you enter the marketplace.

You receive an unsolicited email from a company that just happens to sell something on their website. You were not even thinking about this company or their merchandise. If you click on the link provided and find yourself shopping you have once again allowed someone else to determine your actions, how you are spending your time and maybe even your money.

You come home to a mailbox full of catalogs selling items you didn't even know existed. Were you thinking, "I wonder what stuff I don't have yet that someone will be selling me today?" Probably not, so see the catalogs for what they are, "time and money robbers" and put them directly into the recycling bin.

You feel overworked at your job. You have too much to do and too little time to do it. If you accept the status quo you are allowing others to decide for you how much work you will be doing and how much time you will be spending at work. Practice saying, "I can't do my best work under these circumstances. I'm just one person and I can't do any more. The work will have to wait or be given to someone else." Another option is to ask, "What project should I discontinue or postpone in order to take on this new assignment?" Decide today how much time and energy you want to devote to your job, to your family, to your friends, to relaxation and to entertainment. Set your priorities and stick to them.

You subscribe to the daily newspaper and feel compelled to read all of it. You cut out articles to read "later" and you even attempt to read the back issues when you return from vacation. Newspaper editors decide what to put into each issue of the paper, what stories to include and which interpretations to present. Do you really want to spend your precious time reading everything that someone else decides is newsworthy? Read what interests you and skip the rest. If it's important to know, you'll hear about it from multiple sources.

When you watch TV someone else has chosen for you who will be featured and what topics will be presented. It makes no difference if it's news, information, or entertainment or how many channels you have. Choose wisely.

Your children want to join a sport which practices more often than is realistic for your family schedule and for their ability to keep up with their schoolwork and to just be kids. Speak up! If enough parents complained the sports organizations would be forced to change their ways.

If you respond to phone calls or text messages when they are sent, you have allowed someone else to interrupt your life. Is their message really that urgent or important that you have to stop what you're doing and answer them? If you're already interacting with someone else, how does this behavior appear to the person you're with? Just because we have the technology to be immediately available doesn't mean we need to be. Unless you are expecting an urgent message, turn off your phone and only check for messages when it's convenient for you. That is why we have voice mail!

By being aware, you can take control. Each day, make conscious, informed choices. Live your life your way.

Forget About It Today!
October 2015

Clutter is something you do to yourself. Letting go sounds easy but can be challenging, particularly if you have any perfectionist tendencies. To live a clutter-free life you must be brutally honest with yourself. Admit that you've taken on more than you can handle, that your expectations for yourself are unrealistic and consequently self-defeating. If you always expect too much, you'll be constantly disappointed. Where's the freedom in that? This month I challenge you to pitch whole unfinished projects without looking back, to donate ruthlessly, and to let go of the past to make room for the present. Take three deep breaths and begin!

Here's a list to get you started. Get rid of the easiest first and work up to the harder items. Remember, we're not looking for the "perfect" way to handle these, just the "get-it-done-now-so-you-can-go-live-your-life" way!

Level One: Throw Out!

• The garment with the stubborn stains.

• The barely touched Baby Book for the child who is now researching colleges. New moms don't have time to complete Baby Books. Throw these out and don't give them as gifts, ever!!

• Socks and underwear with holes don't need to be mended; they need to be thrown out.

• Old albums full of photos of people you don't know.

• That half-completed project with an unfixable mistake.

• The cracked vase that leaks.

• The plant that's drooping and will never regain its health.

• Your high school and college notebooks and textbooks.

• The recipes you'll never make.

• Recycle the pile of magazines gathering dust in the corner. You can't read everything.

Level Two: Donate

• The clothing with the tags still on that you'll never wear.

• The clothes you've outgrown.

• The uncomfortable shoes and boots you don't wear.

• The books you'll never read or won't read again.

• Items belonging to the deceased. No amount of keeping the belongings of the deceased can bring them back. Keep your memories of your loved ones and let the rest go.

• Any belongings you don't use or love.

• Collections from a previous chapter in your life.

• Craft supplies, especially those from projects you intended to make but never started.

• Stuff you felt obligated to buy at a house party but never used.

• Something someone gave you that doesn't suit your tastes. "The person is not the thing and the thing is not the person." Keep the friend and let the unloved gift go.

Level Three: Forgive

- Your mistakes
- Your shortcomings
- Others' mistakes and shortcomings

Happy Clutter-free October!

Don't "Should" On Yourself
November 2011

Whenever I speak to a group, I always ask, "If you were told today that you have 6 months to live, how would you spend the time?" Invariably the answers are "travel" and "spend time with family and friends." In the years I've been posing this question, no one has ever said, "I'd run around trying to eat three Thanksgiving meals in one day just to please my relatives," or "I'd stay up all night baking Christmas cookies," or "I'd hurry out to buy a bunch of useless stuff to give as gifts."

If you had six months to live, the time spent with family and friends would involve giving and receiving undivided attention in a meaningful atmosphere. Everyone would try to be on their best behavior, not crabby, frantic, or stressed-out, and you would cherish each precious moment together.

Since we don't know how long we'll live, I suggest structuring your holidays to create an atmosphere of joyful celebration. Imagine that there are no "shoulds" involved, not from yourself or from others. What would your ideal holiday celebration look and feel like? How can you create that new, improved version?

Approach your relatives saying, "Let's try this for one year. If you don't like it, we'll change it back next year." Based on the feedback I get whenever I mention this topic, people are ready for a more manageable approach to their holidays. So be the first, be the role model, and speak up! You might be pleasantly surprised at the response.

Even if you can't convince others to change, you can make new choices regarding your participation. Offer to bring something you can make in advance. Schedule shopping for the ingredients and schedule the baking/cooking now. Put it in your planner and allow plenty of time for do-overs. These are vital appointments you make with yourself to maintain your sanity.

If someone in your family is prone to create procrastination dramas, don't play along. Call them today to start planning. Write down the plans - who's doing what and when? Follow up with an email, as you would in your workplace. Maintain clear participation boundaries. Refuse to take on others' last-minute "emergencies."

With today's blended families, there's a temptation/expectation to attend multiple gatherings in one day. After all, Thanksgiving is technically one day per year. But you can appreciate and celebrate with family at any time. Are your kids growing up believing that Thanksgiving is the most stressful day of the year because inevitably adults end up yelling at each other in the car? What message are you sending about spending time with family? Is it a positive message of loving togetherness or one of dread and obligation?

If you're inclined to expend too much time, energy, and money on decorating for the holidays, stop. People come to your house to see YOU and to enjoy your company, not to see your stuff. In fact, too many decorations are distracting. And too much food is overwhelming. Host a realistic gathering where you're well-rested and cheerful, where you can enjoy yourself and your guests.

Resist the temptation to complain about how busy you are preparing for the holidays. Everyone who's forced to listen to you is thinking, "stop doing all that unnecessary stuff!" A woman approached me after a program and explained that one year, her family members each wrote down the three most important elements of celebrating Christmas. No one mentioned the Christmas tree so they stopped having a tree. This is a wonderful idea that can be applied to any celebration. What aspects of the holiday are the most meaningful to you and your family? What would you miss if it didn't happen or wasn't there? By creating a customized holiday you can maintain what's significant and pare down the rest.

If you're hosting a holiday gathering this month or next, sit down today with a pen and paper and begin planning. What will you serve and on which dishes? What else will you need - tablecloth (does it need ironing?), napkins, plates, silverware, does anything need polishing? How about the table decorations, guest list, house-cleaning? What will you wear and does it need mending or laundering? Think it through, write it down, now! You can think more clearly when you're not last-minute-stressed-out. Planning ahead saves you time, energy, and money.

Find and use what you already have so you won't be tempted to buy more. Be creative with the items currently in your possession. Remember, people are there to see you and to see each other. Perfect decorations are not required. Whatever needs to occur between now and the event, schedule all the steps and put them in your planner as confirmed appointments. Everything you or someone else needs to do such as shopping for ingredients, preparing food, or bathing the dogs! You're much less likely to overextend yourself when you've planned carefully in advance. PLAN stands for Prepare List As Needed.

Everyone has 24 hours in their day, you don't get 25 or 26! You're only one person and you can only do so much. And when you try to do too much, the results aren't favorable. It's impossible to be on your best behavior and truly cherish your time with others when you're sleep-deprived, irritable, angry, frustrated, and/or overwhelmed.

It is possible and preferable to create holidays you look forward to instead of dreading. Stop "shoulding" on yourself, and don't allow others to "should" on you!

Take control. Set clear boundaries. Be realistic. PLAN and enjoy happy, joyful, and memorable holidays!

The Best Presents Aren't Things: Priceless Gifts

December 2012

How can we give meaningful gifts that will show our love and appreciation for others without creating more clutter?

Teachers and Coaches

As a former teacher, I can assure you that teachers don't need any more coffee mugs, ornaments, or items with teaching-related insignias. The best present for a teacher is a heartfelt, hand-written thank-you note. If your handwriting is illegible, type the note and sign it. A woman who attended my "Best Presents Aren't Things" program explained how she personalized her version of this gift. When her kids were little, before they could write their own thank-you notes, she would write whatever they dictated to her. She had them complete a sentence such as "I love you because" and she would write out whatever response her children gave, in their words. This is such a wonderful way to teach your children at an early age how to express their appreciation and the value of doing so. Thank-you notes are read, re-read and treasured!

People Who Can't Easily Go Out

Here's another great idea shared by a class participant. She and her husband arrange to visit people in their neighborhood who are homebound. They bring along a meal, but they also tell the person ahead of time to make a list of small tasks that need to be done around the house. After sharing the meal, the woman and her husband tackle the jobs list - often everyday activities such as getting a box down from an upper shelf or changing a light bulb. They're tasks we take for granted, but that may be difficult, dangerous, or impossible for someone with limited mobility. The recipients are so grateful for the company and the help, and the woman confessed that the experience is just as satisfying for her and her husband! It doesn't take any money or special skills, just some quality time helping their neighbors to create lasting memories for everyone involved.

People Who Can Go Out, But Rarely Do

When my mother was living in assisted living, she had a roommate named Lorraine. Lorraine didn't have many relatives living nearby, so we invited her to spend Christmas Day at our house. I chose a cookie recipe that my mother, Lorraine, and I could make. It's a chocolate-covered-cherry cookie with lots of easy steps. At one point Lorraine said, "This is so much fun! I used to love to bake, but I don't get to do this anymore!" It was true. At the assisted living, everything was done for them including preparing food. Providing the opportunity to perform the simple, beloved task of baking Christmas cookies was Lorraine's favorite gift.

Taking someone to see the holiday lights is a wonderful present for those who can't drive. Stop on the way home for a hot chocolate!

Difficult-to-buy-for Teenager

I assume this is a gift for a teenager you will be seeing at some point. Give the teenager a gift of an hour or two of your uninterrupted time, introducing them to one of your interests. For instance, if you like to golf, take a golf lesson together. If you like the symphony, arrange to attend a concert together including the pre-concert talk introducing the music and soloists. If you love art, take the teenager to an art museum. Show them your favorite artwork and let them choose what else they want to see. Let their mood dictate the type of art to view! If you love to cook or bake, cook or bake together. If you do crafts, create something together. The gift recipient doesn't have to start loving what you love to do, but it will be an opportunity for you to get to know each other as individuals. If you already share an interest, then by all means, focus on that and choose an experience that is above and beyond the usual. For example, if you both love football, attend an event where NFL players are signing autographs. If you both love to ice skate, schedule a skating outing. Set some ground rules like "no phones" and "best behavior" by both of you and enjoy your precious time together! You can also trade an hour of something you choose with an hour of something they want to do with you.

Families

If you have relatives who shower your kids with gifts you don't even want them to have, suggest one of these alternatives: museum or zoo membership, YMCA membership, state park sticker, camping gear, music lessons or music camp, sports lessons or sports camp, ski lift tickets, gift certificates to the theater or symphony, a day at an indoor water park, dance lessons, martial arts membership, ice skates, snow shoes, geo-caching equipment - anything that encourages family togetherness or provides a special experience for a child.

Employees

If you are an employer or manager, have a massage therapist bring a massage chair to your place of employment and give everyone 10-minute neck massages. Sometimes they'll include wax treatments for hands as a bonus. This would be especially good for a PTA to give to ALL the staff at a school. It's affordable and appreciated!

Groups

If your social, church, or professional group typically does an ornament exchange, speak up and remind people that NO ONE needs another ornament! Contact your local school principal or social service agency to buy presents for a needy family. Have your group members bring the wrapped gifts to your December meeting. Or arrange to cook a meal at the local Women's shelter.

Friends

Arrange to do something fun or new together.

Take a class - cooking, decluttering, foreign language, dancing, exercise. Schedule a creative activity - beading, scrapbooking, baking, knitting. Attend a cultural or sports event or just plan a relaxing hike, soaking up the fresh air together. A friend of mine and I recently brought our beads to a women's shelter. We helped the residents create earrings and bracelets to give as Christmas presents. We provided all the supplies including boxes and ribbon so each woman left with several wrapped handmade gifts. This activity proved to be as meaningful for us as it was for them!

For any gift, for any occasion, ask yourself, "What gift would make this person's life a little easier? Bring a smile to their face? Create a lasting memory? Does it need to be a special once-in-a-lifetime experience, an everyday activity or something in between?"

Any time we give our undivided attention, it's a priceless gift. The next time you're talking on the phone, do only that one thing. Talk and listen, nothing else. Notice how much more meaningful and productive the phone call can be. When having a face-to-face conversation, especially with a friend or family member, resist the temptation to interrupt. Let them speak and really listen instead of just waiting your turn!

Give the priceless gift of your time, energy, and attention!

Stories

Life's A Beach
July 2007

6:30 PM Friday

Kay's young daughter Angela loads the dishwasher while Kay begins baking brownies. As the brownies bake, Kay and her daughter gather their swimsuits, towels, sunscreen and the other items they'll need to take to the beach tomorrow.

In another part of town, Jay enters his house carrying a half-eaten sub sandwich. He adds the day's mail to the growing pile on the table and turns on the TV. As he sits down to finish his sandwich, he remembers the big company picnic the next day. He also remembers that he signed up to bring cups. How many was he supposed to bring, he wonders? That number is scribbled on a piece of paper somewhere on the table. He thinks he needs at least 30. He leaves the house again to buy the cups. In the car he decides that 24-ounce heavy-duty blue plastic cups would be perfect.

8:00 PM Friday

Jay is still shopping. One store had the cups but they were in packs of 25. He didn't want to buy 2 packs and have 20 left over. Another store didn't have blue cups. A third store only had the 16-ounce cups. As a last resort, Jay drives across town to the shopping club store. They have the perfect cups, only they are in a huge package of 200. But they are a great price so Jay puts them in his cart. On his way to the checkout, he fills his cart with more stuff. When he checks out, his bill comes to $150. He pays with a credit card.

9:00 PM Friday

Kay reads Angela a story until the girl goes to sleep. Kay frosts the brownies and goes to bed. She reads and dozes until she hears her son, Joshua come home from his summer job at a nearby restaurant. She reminds him to set his alarm since they will be leaving early in the morning. He grumbles a bit but doesn't complain. He knows how important the big company picnic is to his mother. He falls asleep hoping there will be other teenagers there.

10:00 PM Friday

Jay is back home. He leaves his purchases in his car since he'll need the cups in the morning. He turns on the TV and falls asleep.

2:00 AM Saturday

Jay wakes up on the couch with a stiff neck. He crawls into bed exhausted.

7:00 AM Saturday

Kay and her kids finish breakfast. Her daughter cleans off the table as her son helps load the car. Kay checks her list and adds one more item to the cooler.

8:00 AM Saturday

Kay and her family arrive at the beach. She had signed up to help with the set-up so she is glad to see that she is one of the first to arrive. The parking is perfect - close to the picnic shelter and the playground. A car pulls up and parks next to Kay. A young boy jumps out and immediately runs over to the swings. His mother, Joanne introduces herself and is surprised when Kay introduces Joshua as her son. She thinks, she looks too young to have a son that age! Joshua and Kay help Joanne unload her car as Angela heads for the swings.

9:00 AM Saturday

Jay awakens as the sun streams in the window. He looks at the clock and remembers the picnic. He skips breakfast, planning to get something to eat at the drive - thru where he buys his coffee. All week, he has spent his evenings researching the Web for new sand castle designs and now he can't find the print-outs he made. He searches through the piles of papers on his desk, on the table, in the living room. After 45 minutes, he gives up the search. He begins to fill his car with everything he can think of to bring. He's determined to make the biggest, most elaborate sand castle ever! It's after 10 AM when he finally leaves. Halfway there he realizes he forgot sunscreen so he stops to buy some.

As others arrive with the food and beverages, Kay and Joanne watch their young children playing.

Joanne does not recognize Kay and asks her about her position with the company. Kay tells Joanne how much she loves working for the company but confides that she's not sure how long she can stay without having more flexible hours. With Joshua going away to college in the fall, Kay will need to be home by the time Angela gets out of school in the afternoons.

11:00 AM Saturday

The picnic is in full swing. Jay has made a second stop, this time at the hobby shop to buy one more mold for his sand castle. He is the last person to arrive at the picnic and has to park at the far end of the beach. Because he has so much gear to haul, he sets up near his car far away from the picnic shelter.

12:00 PM Saturday

Jay remembers the cups and takes them to the picnic area. There is a table with plates, napkins, and open packages containing every size and color of cups. Everyone else has had their first helping of food and some are going back for seconds. Kay sees

Jay walking down the beach carrying the huge package of cups and recognizes him from the pictures of the employee of the month. She walks over and thanks him for bringing the cups, but points out to him that they already have enough cups. She suggests that he take his cups back to the car so he can return them to the store. She is just trying to be helpful, but Jay chooses to be offended by her remarks. How dare she not recognize how perfect my cups are, he thinks.

1:00 PM Saturday

Jay takes a plate of food and the cups back to his spot at the other end of the beach and begins to build his sand castle. As he digs and molds the sand, a few people walk by. Three of his co-workers invite him to join the volleyball game, but he declines. He's afraid to leave all his stuff unattended and he worries that someone could ruin his castle while he's away.

Kay's son Joshua has met some other teenagers who are helping the younger children create a sand castle city near the picnic area. Since her kids are occupied, Kay decides to join the volleyball game. A co-worker comments that she saw Kay talking to Joanne, who is one of the senior vice-presidents. Kay did not realize who Joanne was, and recalls their conversation. Oh well, she thinks, I said what I truly believe. I do love my job and I also need more flexible hours to properly care for my daughter.

2:00 PM

Kay sits on the beach a short distance from the group reading her book while her daughter plays nearby. A small dog runs up to Kay with a stick in its mouth and drops it at her feet. Kay picks up the stick and throws it into the water. The dog runs and swims after it, returning for more play. Kay plays fetch with the dog until it loses interest and wanders down the beach.

Jay is engrossed in his sand castle. It's quite elaborate with large turrets and multiple levels. He thinks, it's too bad so few people have bothered to come over to see it. A small dog walks by, sniffs at one of the castle corners and lifts its leg. Jay looks around to see that no one has noticed and covers the spot with a fresh coat of sand.

3:00 PM

Dark clouds appear as thunder rumbles in the distance. Tired and well-fed, Kay and her family members join the others in packing their cars to return home.

Jay has been so busy digging into the sand that he doesn't realize he's now standing in a fairly deep hole. While building his castle, he completely surrounded himself in the process. As the storm approaches, he debates how to extract himself without ruining his hard work. In the end, he creates a bridge and a new opening on one side which allows him to step out without harming the rest of the structure.

SATURDAY EVENING

As Kay drifts off to sleep she has the same thought she's had for years, "Thank you for my children and for this wonderful day!"

As Joanne puts her son to bed she thinks, "Kay is right, flexible hours would allow all the employees to spend more time with their children or other family members in their care. I'll talk to the president of the company on Monday."

As Jay sits down at his computer he wonders how much his castle was damaged by the rain.

11:00 PM

The tide comes in and washes away all the castles. After all, they were only made of sand!

Are you building sand castles or a fulfilling life?

Fall Colors
October 2008

9:00 PM Friday

Kay's young daughter, Angela fills the water bottles and puts them in the refrigerator. Kay's son, Joshua who has been away at college, is home for the weekend to participate in the bike ride the next day. He pumps up the tires, then helps his mother load the bikes into the car as they discuss the pledges they collected for the annual fund-raising event. Kay reminds her children to set out their jackets in case it's cold in the morning. They agree to set their alarms for 6:00 AM and head off to their respective rooms for a good night's sleep.

In another part of town, Jay enters his house carrying packages from the bike store. He looks around for a place to put them, then shrugs and drops them on the floor near the door. He hasn't eaten dinner. He opens the refrigerator only to find 2 slices of pizza sitting uncovered on a plate and some expired milk. He searches through the piles of paper on the kitchen counter trying to find the phone number of any restaurant that delivers. He sees an old menu on the floor and picks it up, but realizes it's from a place that went out of business over a year ago. After more searching he finds the phone book and calls to order dinner.

10:30 PM Friday
Jay finishes eating while watching TV. He thinks about the bike ride the next day and wonders if his new bike jersey will be warm enough. He doesn't want to cover it up with a jacket.

7:00 AM Saturday
Kay, Angela, and Joshua finish breakfast. They take their chilled water bottles and jackets and head out the door.

Jay awakens and begins thinking about last year's bike ride. He gets mad all over again about the person who rode too close and put a tiny scratch in his bike frame. This year, he's determined to stay in the front of the pack with the racers who he's sure will respect his bike and admire his new jersey. As he looks for his water bottle, he notices that one of his tires is flat. He attempts to inflate it, then decides to change it instead. By this time it's getting late. He rushes out the door without eating breakfast. When he arrives at the event, he has to park at the farthest lot, hurrying to register in time. He is given a T-shirt and number to wear which he reluctantly puts on over his bike jersey. It's too late to get to the front of the group, so he is forced to line up in back with the other latecomers.

8:30AM Saturday

The ride is under way with several thousand people taking part. The atmosphere is convivial. Kay breathes in the crisp fall air and is grateful for her children's presence and their good health. She jokes with her son and watches as her daughter gains confidence riding in the group. Everyone around them is enjoying the beautiful day and feeling good about supporting a worthy cause.

Meanwhile Jay is trying to pass people to get to the front. He notices a co-worker and wonders how she can afford such an expensive bike. Suddenly, everywhere he looks, it seems that everyone else has a nicer bike than he. He wonders if he has enough availability on his credit card to buy a new bike and decides to visit the bike store on his way home. Because he isn't watching where he's going, he nearly crashes into another rider. He thinks, "If I take vacation days next year at this time, my boss can't make me ride in this." He spends the rest of the ride plotting how to avoid it in the future. He's a little more careful as he passes the other bicyclists and he gets to the front just as the ride is ending. He is out of breath, hungry, tired, and crabby. He rides back to his car alone.

12:30 PM Saturday
At the end of the ride, Kay and her kids join the others for the lunch that is provided. They sit under a maple tree ablaze with fall colors. They are tired, content, happy, and fulfilled.

Which character are you most like?
Kay or Jay?

Change Your Mind

Forgiveness
April 2013

Whether through a lifetime of accumulation or a short-term change of lifestyle, people arrive at their clutter due to many circumstances. One person feels the effects of clutter when a spouse dies and suddenly, there's too much stuff to deal with. Another person is overwhelmed by their children's overstuffed toy bins. A seemingly "organized" person can overbook themselves and experience a cluttered calendar. Each person and situation is unique.

After years of working with people and their clutter, I have seen one common element - a lack of forgiveness - forgiveness of others and most importantly, forgiveness of self. Lack of forgiveness keeps us stuck in old thought and behavior patterns and consequently prevents us from letting go of the related belongings.

Clutter-free living requires you to tell yourself the unvarnished truth. Forgiving doesn't mean you condone a particular behavior, it just means you are ready to set yourself free from the result of that behavior.

If you felt deprived as a child, forgive your parents for their inability to provide for your needs. No amount of buying excess stuff now can fix what occurred long ago. Forgive yourself for trying to fill an emotional hole with physical belongings and see your belongings as the inanimate objects they are.

Forgive your spouse for dying. Keeping the belongings of the deceased won't bring him or her back. You're still here, so how are you going to live the next chapter of your life - one that doesn't include the deceased person? What stuff do you honestly need to live this new chapter to its fullest? If you had died, would you want your surviving spouse to save all of your stuff and stay stuck in the past? Hopefully not!

Forgive yourself for attaching your self-worth to what you own. We're constantly bombarded by marketing that tells us we're only as valuable as our next new purchase, whether it's the latest phone, car, house, or pair of shoes. See that for what it is - an insidious lie designed to fatten someone else's bank account while it drains yours. Forgive others for getting sucked into the hype and free yourself from this line of thinking. Your belongings are meant to serve you, not enslave you or define you. The truth is that you are sacred and priceless, regardless of what you own.

Forgive yourself for your mistakes. If you bought things for your fantasy body or your fantasy life, tell the truth, learn from your mistakes and let the items go. We all make mistakes, it's part of living.

If you've committed to doing more than is humanly possible and now you're feeling crabby and stressed out about it, forgive yourself and cancel something. You're only one person with the same 24-hour day as everyone else on the planet. Forgive others for being momentarily upset or disappointed. They will eventually be glad to be around the happier version of you, once you're giving yourself a more realistic schedule!

Forgive the world for changing faster than you prefer. Forgive yourself for not keeping up.

Forgive your parents for what they taught you or failed to teach you. You're an adult now and can choose your own beliefs and actions.

Forgive your friends for giving you presents you neither need nor want. Forgive yourself for making emotional attachments to stuff. If you don't love it, let it go.

Forgive yourself and everyone around you for not being perfect. No one is!

If you bought more than you can manage and keep track of, take a good long look at your shopping habits. Forgive yourself and set upon a new course.

Take a new road on your journey of life and practice new habits, with less cluttered results.

Forgive others and yourself for being stuck in old ways of thinking and behaving. You can't change others, but you can be a shining example for the positive benefits of change. Be brave, be the first!

Don't waste another minute of your life regretting the past or ruminating about it. You can't change the past. You CAN change your mind, you can choose to forgive, and you can move forward with a loving heart and a lot less stuff.

Begin today!

Someday Is Not a Day of the Week!

June 2013

"I have to keep this in case I might need it someday" is a phrase that could potentially be applied to just about anything anyone can own. But does it really make any sense?

If you have any spiritual or religious beliefs, you believe you have divine help here on earth. That's common among all spiritual practices. If you claim to believe that you have help on your earthly journey, but you say "I have to keep this in case I might need it someday," that's a contradiction. If you need something, it will show up or another way to accomplish a task will appear. If you really have the beliefs you claim, then prove it by your actions.

If you keep a lot of stuff from the past, you have to put your energy into maintaining the memories of the past. If you keep things in case you might need them someday, you're projecting your energy into the future and speculating about the future. That leaves little energy for the present, but we live in the present. Keep only what you need for your current life. Keep only as much as you have room for and can keep track of.

If you lost everything in a tornado, what would you replace?

There are only two options.
Make progress or make excuses.

The Truth About Clutter
Oct 2011

Warning: This newsletter contains the unvarnished TRUTH about your clutter. Brace yourself!

Did you wake up this morning, look around your cluttered home and ask, "Who filled up my house when I was asleep?" Probably not! You know who's responsible for the clutter. Clutter is something you do to yourself. This is good news because it means you can clean it up.

If your environment is as cluttered as it was last week, last month, or last year, it's because you haven't done anything to change it.

No one forced you to clog your home with more stuff than it was designed to hold.

No one forced you to make emotional attachments to inanimate objects.

No one forced you to create piles of unread magazines and newspapers.

No one forced you to acquire more belongings than you can keep track of.

No one forced you to buy clothes you don't wear.

No one forced you to commit to doing more than is humanly possible.

No one forced you to allow your children to have more toys than they can play with.

No one forced you to keep the belongings of deceased relatives.

No one forced you to throw your clothes on the floor.

No one forced you to let your laundry pile up.

No one forced you to waste time in front of the TV or computer screen.

No one is forcing you to procrastinate.

AND

No one is preventing you from decluttering.

No one is preventing you from making new choices.

No one is preventing you from living a clutter-free life.

It's time to quit feeling sorry for yourself, stop making excuses, and start taking charge of your life. It doesn't even matter what circumstances led to the clutter. All that matters is what new steps you take TODAY toward decluttering.

Whenever someone asks me if I've seen a TV show about clutter I immediately think, "Turn off the TV, set your timer for an hour and clean out something - a drawer, a closet, a shelf!" And don't tell me you're too tired. The very act of decluttering will energize you once you start. But that's the key - you must begin.

Take out your planner right now and schedule at least three decluttering sessions of 20 minutes each. When you make an appointment with a doctor or dentist, do you keep that appointment? Of course you do! So give yourself the same courtesy you extend to others and keep those decluttering appointments.

What do you really want to do in life? Which of your many talents is the world missing out on because your clutter is holding you back? Stop allowing your belongings to suck out your life force. Clear the clutter and unleash your true potential.

Today is a brand new day. Now is the perfect time.

Helpful People
March 2010

Living with a lot of clutter can isolate you physically, emotionally, and socially. However, we all depend upon many others as we go about our daily lives. Think of the Olympics and everyone who worked for years to prepare for that event. From those who built the venues to the volunteers who staffed them, thousands of people were involved. For every athlete who competed, there were sponsors, clothing designers, equipment manufacturers, coaches, family, friends, and fans.

This month, practice noticing all the people who work in your behalf. The more clutter you have and the more isolated you feel, the more essential this exercise is for you. Turn off your alarm and recognize that someone designed and made that alarm clock, not to torture you, but to assist you in getting up on time. If there is hot water when you take your shower, be grateful for all the people who keep your electricity flowing. As you eat your cereal, think about the people who own the farmland, plant the seeds, harvest the grains, transport the grains, own the cereal company, work for the cereal company, drive the delivery truck, service the truck, own the grocery store, stock the shelves, design and manufacture the grocery bags, work as check-out clerks, bag your groceries, and wish you a nice day! Then think about the milk on your cereal and how it got there. Think about the bowl and the spoon. Hundreds, if not thousands of people contribute their efforts so you can enjoy your bowl of cereal knowing that it's nourishing and safe to eat.

Every minute of your day is influenced by many many people, most of whom you will never know. You don't need to know them personally to appreciate their contributions to your life.

Celebrate your interconnectedness and acknowledge your own contribution to the lives of others.

My Parents Never Taught Me That!

September 2013

I was 9 years old, waiting for a friend in the kitchen of her house. I remember noticing several days-worth of dirty dishes piled on the counter along with open boxes of cereal. I didn't understand why the family members hadn't put away the cereal. And I wondered why they didn't at least rinse the dishes, even if they couldn't wash them right away. Decades later, while visiting the same friend as an adult with children of her own, I observed the same behavior and result.

Many times, I've had clients state that they are incapable of doing something because their parents never taught them how to do it. This has included handling money, cleaning the house, maintaining order, preparing meals and raising children, to name a few. While it's reasonable to expect that parents will provide their children with basic life skills, that is not always the case. Your parents could only teach you what they, themselves knew how to do, and sometimes, because of extenuating circumstances, they may have been unable to accomplish even that much.

I loved my parents dearly, and I know they did what they thought was best for me. But if I only lived my life based on what they were able to teach me, I would have never gone to college and I would still think that mini-wieners in a tater tot casserole is a fancy dish!

If you think about it, you'll realize that you have acquired many skills on your own over the years. If you're reading this newsletter via email, you probably learned how to transmit and receive email without your parents' help. In fact, you may be the one instructing your parents in this regard.

Consider your parents' teachings as your starting point. It's your job as an adult to further your own education in whatever area needs work. This is easier to do than ever before. There are YouTube videos on every conceivable subject including how to clean your house, along with plenty of Internet blogs dispensing useful advice on daily living.

Even if you're not raising kids, the anticipation of a new school year is in the air. As children return to school and daily life returns to a familiar routine, it's a great time for anyone to make changes that will bring new results.

Do your dishes pile up on the counter because clean dishes are languishing in the dishwasher? How long does it take to empty your dishwasher? Time yourself! It only takes a few minutes to get a clutter-free result.

Do you want to get rid of clutter on the floor? Here's my favorite phrase. Repeat aloud as often as needed. "Floors are for feet and furniture and furry animals" - assuming you have a pet! If you don't throw your belongings on the floor in the first place, you won't have that mess to clean up later.

Plan your meals for the week and shop with a detailed list. Only buy what you need. Avoid the temptation to walk up and down every aisle.

Schedule decluttering appointments with yourself and keep those appointments!

It's time to stop blaming your parents for your shortcomings. Grow up and show up.

Too Many Rules!

Feb 2014

We all grew up with rules. We followed the rules, ignored them, and/or rebelled against them. Sports have rules. Religions have rules. Schools have rules. Businesses have rules. Clubs have rules. Cities, states, and countries have rules. Families have rules. As a society, we need some rules to function.

What rules have you created for yourself? What rules created by others are you following? Do they enhance your life? Do they waste your time, money and/or energy? Are they outdated or just plain silly? Are you following any of these rules?

• Kitchen towels must be ironed.
• You can't start to declutter until you have the right bins.
• Get rid of anything you haven't used in a year.
• You must own the newest smartphone.
• Grey hair must be dyed and covered up.
• If it's on sale, buy it.

- Believe everything you hear on the radio/TV.
- You must buy books recommended by others.
- White pants can only be worn in summer.
- Baskets are required for organizing.
- You must own shoes to match every outfit.
- To be organized, watch organizing TV shows and read organizing magazines.
- Always take whatever is offered to you.
- Women over 50 can't wear short skirts.
- If it's "buy-one-get-one-half-price" you must buy two.
- If it comes in the mail, you must read it before throwing it out.
- You can't move until you've packed up everything perfectly.
- Keep greeting cards forever.
- The more organizing books you own, the more organized you'll be.
- Always carry the latest style/color of purse.
- Your "family heirlooms" must stay in your family, even if no one wants them.
- You must take your phone everywhere and answer every call.

- Save every recipe that interests you.
- Clip all coupons.
- You must care about what others think of you.
- Keep all items in a set (cookware, plastic containers, dishes, etc.) even if you don't use them, in case you ever donate them.
- Put all your receipts in a large bin and save them, just in case...
- Shop frequently at second hand stores and rummage sales.
- You must read every email.
- When grocery-shopping, you have to go up and down every aisle.
- If it comes in three colors you have to buy all three.
- If you can't do it perfectly, don't start.
- If you can't do everything perfectly, feel guilty.
- You're too young to do that.
- You're too old to change.
- Never pay full price.
- Own every year's power company Cookie Book even if you don't bake.
- You can't wear nice clothes until you lose weight.

• You have to check your phone/email as soon as you awaken.

• Research all possible options before making a purchasing decision, even for something as mundane as a toaster.

• You have to start each day with coffee.

• At your age, your options are limited.

• Always eat everything on your plate.

• You have to say "Yes" even when you're already too busy.

When it comes to decluttering and living your best version of a clutter-free life, here's my advice in the form of my favorite quote:

"There are no rules here, we're trying to accomplish something."   Thomas Edison

Barking Dogs
October 2012

In our old neighborhood lived an energetic dog named Buddy. When Buddy was a puppy, he would enthusiastically greet everyone who walked past his house. In response, his parents had an invisible fence installed so Buddy could no longer run into the road. Instead, Buddy began to bark his greetings. Unfortunately, Buddy barked from the time he saw someone enter his field of vision until after they disappeared. Because of the position of his house on his circular street, Buddy had plenty of time to bark! His parents never learned to control Buddy. They would apologize to passers-by about the barking and meekly plead with Buddy to stop barking, to no avail. Then one day, we walked past Buddy's house when he was outside. He barked, but this time it sounded faint and garbled as if he had laryngitis. On subsequent walks, his bark was still weak and much softer. Instead of learning how to train and control their dog, it appeared that Buddy's parents took drastic measures to minimize the volume of his bark.

What drastic measures have you taken to try to control your clutter? It seems to me that clutter is very much like a barking dog to which you're emotionally attached and feel powerless to control. If you have more clothes than will fit into your closet, extender bars on the outside or expensive closet inserts are the equivalent of surgery to control barking. They don't address the real problem that you have too many clothes - more clothes than you can manage. The truth is you need to learn how to live with less. Start by getting rid of or packing away everything you don't LOVE. Get used to seeing a reasonable amount of clothing in your closet. Do the same with your drawers. Next, deal with your shoes.

Instead of limiting the amount of wrapping paper you own, have you purchased gigantic, unwieldy bins to hold it all? Or have you set up a "wrapping station" in your home as if you're in the business of wrapping presents on a daily basis? What other explanation can there be for such a ridiculous use of time, energy, and space? I've been in homes where there is more wrapping paper than at the paper store! Keep a few rolls of solid color wrapping paper and donate the rest to your local school's art teacher.

Instead of making decisions to get rid of the stuff you neither need nor use, have you stuffed your basement to the rafters? Do you keep things in case you might need them someday?

Be truthful with yourself and admit that you really couldn't find that stuff if and when you would need it, so let it all go. You've lived perfectly well for years without having access to any of it, so clearly you don't need it.

Instead of paring down to a manageable amount of belongings, have you pined for a larger dwelling, built an addition to your existing space, or added more furniture that holds stuff? How about only owning what your dwelling was designed to hold?

If you start to see your clutter as that barking dog, what new tactics could you employ? How can you train yourself to be satisfied with less? Just be honest with yourself. Begin by remembering that clutter is something you do to yourself and vow to undo it. Make a distinction between what you want (everything!) and what you need to have a functional life.

Too much of anything over-complicates your life. So tell yourself, I want that, but I sure don't need that, therefore I'm going to choose to make better use of my time, energy, and money. Before you buy another bin or organizing system, ask yourself, "If it all blew away in a tornado, how much would I replace?" Your answer will help you see how little you really need to have a full life!

More isn't better, more is just more, and too much is clutter.

You Can't Take it With You
June 2008

Recently, I met a woman who was planning to move across the country to start a new chapter in her life. A relative of hers had suggested that instead of spending lots of time packing and loads of money moving, she should just take her personal belongings and clothes and buy everything else she needed when she arrived at her new home. I thought about the times we moved and how much money we paid moving companies to haul our stuff. For some of the items, we've certainly spent more to move them than we did to acquire them! Whether or not you have any intention to move, this is an intriguing way to evaluate your belongings.

Pretend you are about to move. Walk around your home looking closely at everything you own. Ask yourself for each item, "Would I miss this or replace this if I moved without taking it?" What would you buy instead, or would you do without it? This is a great way to re-evaluate the number of each item you own. For example, if you were furnishing a kitchen, how many dishes, glasses, mugs, pots and pans would you need? If you were furnishing bedrooms, how many sets of bedding would you need? Use your answers to these questions as motivation to declutter and pare down.

When I was trying this re-evaluating exercise in my own home, I was surprised to discover how many things I would neither miss nor replace. It was a good way to determine which items I really love, whether they were given as gifts or purchased. It made me realize once again that I don't need a lot of stuff to be happy.

When my husband and I vacation in Europe, we rent a small apartment. They tend to have one bedroom, a galley kitchen, a bathroom, and a room for living/dining all in about 400-500 square feet. I have often contemplated what life would be like if this was where we lived full-time. Having more space and more stuff does not automatically translate into a better life!

One aspect of my work with clients is getting all items in one category into one space in the house. It's important to know the quantity of items when we're creating a place for them to live. When my clients see how much of an item they have, such as wrapping paper, they often remark about how much money the stuff represents. A few dollars here and there really adds up, and pretty soon you have more wrapping paper than you can use in a lifetime! Sometimes, they're reluctant to get rid of something, even though they aren't using it, because of how much they paid for it! Don't let this deter you from releasing the things you don't need or use. You can't change what you spent in the past, but you can change how you spend from now on.

Use this pretend-move exercise to think about the total amount of money you want to spend on each category of stuff in your life. If you were starting from scratch, would you set new standards for your purchases? Would you be more inclined to buy only the things you love? Would you stop yourself after you bought what you needed or would you keep shopping? You don't need to wait until you move. At any time, you can adopt new standards for shopping. I'm not suggesting that you get rid of everything and buy all new. But the next time you think you need to add another thing to your home or life, stop and re-think the purchase. Ask yourself, "What 3 or 4 things will I get rid of to make way for the new one?"

How much stuff do you really need to live a full and satisfying life? How much time and money do you want to spend acquiring stuff?

How do you want to spend your life?

Want vs. Need: Which One is Winning in Your Life?

August 2012

If you've ever interacted with a child, you have heard them say emphatically, "I don't want to do that!" or "I want that!" As the adult in the situation, it's easy to see that what the child wants and what they need are two different things. And as the adult, you are likely to see to it that the child does or receives what is needed, overriding what is wanted.

How often in your life do you proclaim your wants, completely ignoring the corresponding and often contradictory need?

Here are some examples to consider.

I want to sit in this chair and read all day, but I need to go to the park and play with my granddaughter.

I want to go out to lunch with my co-workers, but I need to bring a healthy lunch and eat outside.

I want to stay up all night and finish this project, but I need to go to bed and get some sleep so I'm not grumpy tomorrow.

I want to employ all manner of excuses, but I need to see possibilities and make new choices.

I don't want to eat fruit and vegetables, but I need to do so in order to be healthy.

I want to have some fun, but I need to tend to my mail and cleaning first.

I want to be judgmental, but I need to be grateful instead.

I want to bring work home on the weekends, but I need to have more balance in my life.

My kids want to join lots of activities, but we need to eat dinner together as a family.

I want to identify with my belongings, but I need to see myself as worthy with or without them.

I want to ruminate about past events, but I need to focus my energy and attention on the present.

I want to spend my time on Social Media websites, but I need to get out of the house and interact with people face-to-face.

I want to procrastinate, then say I didn't have enough time, but I need to take responsibility for my actions and complete my work.

I want to wash down my lunch with a super-sized soft drink, but I need to choose to drink water instead.

I want to drive a fancy car, but I need to pay off my mortgage.

I want to do everything myself, my way, but I need to ask for help and allow others to assist me.

I want to do two more things before I leave the house, but I need to show respect for others and arrive on time.

I want a closet makeover, but I just need to donate the clothes I don't wear.

I want to stay up late watching a movie, but I need to go to bed now so I get enough sleep.

I want to check my messages as soon as I get up in the morning, but I need to have clearer boundaries between work & personal time.

I want to use my volunteering as an excuse ("I'm too busy"), but I need to create a realistic schedule for myself.

I want to hit the snooze alarm, but I need to get up and exercise.

I want to treat myself to a pedicure, but I need to save money for a vacation.

I want to stay in my house, but I need to move to a facility where I'll have help.

I want to eat another piece of pie, but I sure don't need to!!

I want to read that pile of magazines, but I need to cancel the subscriptions and put the unread magazines in the recycling bin.

I want to wait until I can clean perfectly, but I just need to get busy and clean up this mess.

I want to use child-rearing as an excuse ("I'm too busy"), but I need to commit to a schedule of handling the laundry and mail.

I want another glass of wine, but I need to drink less to remain healthy.

I want to buy a shed, but I just need to schedule time to clean out the garage.

I want to shop, but I don't need more of anything.

I don't want to quit smoking, but I need to do so to improve my health.

I want to proclaim, "That's just how I am!" but I need to embrace change.

I don't want to floss my teeth, but I need to do so in order to have teeth!

I want to say the first thing that enters my mind, but I need to take a breath and think before responding.

I don't want to cut back on caffeine, but I need to do so in order to calm down and relax.

I want to blame others, the economy, society for my problems, but I need to use my time/energy to find the solutions that work for me.

I want to go out to eat every weekend, but I need to save money for retirement.

I want to revise that document 3 more times, but I need to recognize that it's good enough and go be with my family.

My aging parents want to stay in their home, but I need to intervene because they are no longer making good choices.

I want to troll the aisles of the craft store, but I need to finish the projects I've already begun.

I want to be a good employee and take on extra projects at work, but I need to say "No, I'm only one person and I can only do so much."

I want to take offense at what others do or say, but I need to see we are all trying to do our best.

I want to interact with my phone, but I need to communicate with the person I'm with.

I want to live as my parents did, but I need to upgrade my thinking & behavior for life in today's world.

I don't want to admit my mistakes, but I need to do so in order to learn from them and move on.

I want to believe that my possessions are somehow special, but I need to see them as the inanimate objects they are, and break free.

I want to wait for the perfect conditions to de-clutter, but I need to begin in some small way TODAY!

Choose to override one "want" and do what you "need" to do instead.   Enjoy the results!

Clean Slate
September 2014

Do you remember how you felt as a child, preparing for the school year to begin? How much time did you spend wondering about your teacher, your classmates, where you would sit, and what would be taught? Did you enter the school building on the first day wearing a new outfit and new shoes?

There was a freshness to the new year, excitement, anticipation, and the feeling of a clean start, unencumbered by the previous year's mistakes and challenges. As adults, we rarely give ourselves or others the gift of a fresh start. Even on January first, we're more inclined to choose New Year's resolutions that focus on our perceived shortcomings.

This month give yourself a clean slate, a fresh start. Let go of the past and its hold over you. Say good-bye to "what if" and "if only." You can't change the past but you can forgive yourself and others and move forward. Grudges bind you to the past. Holding onto belongings that invoke sad or unpleasant memories depletes your energy for positive change. Thoughts of past failures distract you from recognizing present possibilities.

Evaluate your life through compassionate eyes. Admit that you shop too much and too often and start saving for that vacation you say you want to take. Tell the truth about your cluttered schedule and learn to say, "No." You're giving yourself more to do than you can or will do. Only take on the projects and belongings you can manage. Stop expecting yourself to be perfect and realize that we're all human. We make mistakes and we carry on.

Start to notice how often you ruminate about past events. "She said this, and he did that, and I didn't like it, and blah, blah, blah, blah blah." What a colossal waste of time and energy. Catch yourself in this unproductive thought loop, switch gears and think, "What can I do right now to move one step closer to my goals and dreams? Which of my belongings support my journey?"

Remember to give your family and friends a fresh start, too. It's not fair to repeatedly judge others through the filter of past mistakes and old wounds. See your loved ones clearly as they are today. Fully appreciate them for their uniqueness, their accomplishments, the contributions they make to your life.

Learn from nature. Flowers bloom anew each year. Butterflies emerge from cocoons and continue the cycle of life. Animals prepare for winter without regrets about summer. Nature moves forward one step at a time, without remorse or longing for the past.

Letting go of the past creates space for the new to flow in. Start today!

Experience vs. Stuff
August 2010

While we may be inclined to unfavorably compare our belongings to others', we rarely do so with our experiences. A recent study reports that people are more satisfied when they spend money on experiences, such as vacations, than when they spend money on material possessions, such as souvenirs.

Think about an enjoyable trip you've taken. Do you remember the stuff you bought, or are you conjuring up fond memories of the experiences you had? The same can be said for everyday living. We are happiest when we place our attention on enjoying the events of our lives.

Suppose you want to have a picnic but you don't have picnic plates or glasses. No problem! Use your everyday dishes for your picnic, whether it's in your backyard or a park. No special gear is needed to enjoy the experience of eating outside and socializing with friends. There is so much advertising of outdoor dining stuff, you may have forgotten that people have been going on picnics for generations without it. Perhaps you already own special picnic items but haven't used them. Your purchase of the items indicates your desire to have the experience of outdoor dining, so schedule a picnic or cookout for the near future.

The more stuff you have for any occasion, the more storage space you need for it when it's not in use. Before you buy any specialty item, ask yourself how often you will use it. Consider if it's worth the time, energy, and money to procure it and own it. Is there anything you already own that could be used instead? How much stuff do you want to be in charge of?

Now, go have some fun!

Change Your Behavior

5 a Day! No, Not Vegetables!
January 2011

Start off your new year, with a new behavior! Practice it today and every day this year. Simple, yet transformational. Each day, take five minutes to plan for the NEXT day. Start right now.

What do you need to do tomorrow? When do you need to be somewhere and when will you need to leave in order to arrive on time? What will you wear? What do you need to bring? If you can, set those items aside right now. Do you shop for the food and prepare the meals? If so, what will you serve tomorrow and do you have the ingredients, or do you need to buy something for the meal? Are there bills that need to be paid? If so, schedule that bill-paying now. Decide when you will do it and put it in your planner. When will you exercise tomorrow? When will you go to bed in order to get enough rest? Are you responsible for other family members and their activities? Do you share your life with another adult? If so include them in your daily 5-minute planning session.

Think about the frantic moments of your life, whether they occur daily or occasionally. They can be avoided or minimized with pre-planning. If you know what you're going to eat for dinner and you're sure you have the ingredients, there's no need to panic at mealtime. If your kids have to be driven somewhere and you've planned ahead, you can even bring along something to read while you're waiting for them. By reviewing the next day's plan in advance, you'll avoid the arguments that occur when you each assume, incorrectly, that the other person is going to pick up the kids! When you're planning the day before, you'll see alternative solutions. You'll also see when your "schedule" is completely unworkable and needs to be changed!

Do your own experiment and try this for one month. Remember that you are practicing a new behavior. Don't expect perfection, just steady improvement.

Spend 5 minutes today planning; wake up tomorrow knowing you're ready for the day!

A Place for One Thing
Feb 2010

You've probably heard the saying "a place for everything and everything in its place." It might seem impossible, but all you need to do is start with just one item. This month, practice creating and using a space for one frequently-used item. Think of something you use every day or almost every day that you often misplace. It might be your keys, your glasses, your wallet, your purse, your phone, or something else. Whatever comes to mind, choose that item. Resist the temptation to ruminate over this choice to find the "perfect" item. Just choose one thing, right now!

Next, think about how and where you use this item. At home, when you leave the house, at your desk, multiple locations or just one? Picture yourself using the item. Now choose a location for the item to "live" when it isn't in use. Ideally, it will live someplace close to where it is used, some convenient location. Again, it doesn't need the perfect home it just needs an assigned spot to live.

Choose the spot where it will live and move the item into that spot now. Every time you use the item, return it to its designated home as soon as you are finished using it. For this first exercise, pick an item that is used by you alone, not something you share with others.

Here are some examples to help you decide where common items might live. If you frequently misplace your purse, decide to keep in on the shelf in your front hall closet. Whenever you need something from the purse, take it off the shelf and retrieve the item. When you are done interacting with the purse, put it back on the closet shelf. When you come home, put your purse on the closet shelf immediately. Another safe place to keep your purse is in a drawer or cabinet in your dining room. Keys can live on hooks near the door, in a dish on the counter, in a kitchen drawer or in your purse. Checkbooks can live in a desk drawer, a kitchen drawer, or a dresser drawer. Glasses can live in a glass case that is kept on a bathroom shelf, on a nightstand, on your desk, or around your neck on a chain! There is no correct place for these common items to live. Anywhere you choose that you can access regularly will suffice. Pick a place for the item to live that is convenient and logical. Make it as easy as possible for yourself to complete this task.

Don't expect perfection. Keep practicing putting away this one item until it becomes your habit. It takes 21-28 days to develop a new habit, so if you start today, by the end of the month you will always know right where to find this one item and your days of searching for it will be over.

Choose the next item and repeat until everything has an assigned spot to live.

From Fantasy to Truth to Solutions
March 2013

Everywhere you look, you can see ads depicting the fantasy of spring - short sleeve tops, lightweight skirts, pants and polo shirts in jelly bean colors, people playing outdoors. The truth is that Southeastern Wisconsin's average March temperatures are a high of 42 and a low of 27, with 7 inches of snow! April's average temps are a high of 54, low of 37, with an additional 2 inches of snow. Jackets, scarves, and gloves will continue to be worn and the need for closets full of warm-weather clothing is debatable. The stores are trying their best to distract you from the truth. Before you get sucked into a buying frenzy, stop to notice what is motivating you. Will buying new lightweight clothes change our weather? Do you need something new or just a respite from winter? Are there ways to get that respite without adding to your bulging closet? It's easy to get caught up in the fantasy of spring because we wish it were true.

In the same way, you can get caught up in the fantasy version of your life instead of admitting the truth about your belongings - how you acquired them and why you're keeping stuff you don't use.

Here are some examples.

Fantasy: You'll be able to wear decades-old clothes as soon as you lose weight.
Truth: They're not in style and they'll never fit you again.
Solution: Let them go.

Fantasy: You'll finish your son's baby book soon.
Truth: Your son's daughter is planning her wedding!
Solution: Throw out the unfinished baby book!

Fantasy: You'll sell all the cool stuff in your garage on eBay.
Truth: It's been in there for years and you're not sure what you have, what it's worth, or who would want any of it. You've had no time to deal with it recently

because you're too busy calling yourself a "packrat" and acquiring more stuff.

Solution: Stay away from estate and rummage sales. Donate what you have and park your cars in your garage.

Fantasy: You'll host the perfect summer cookout, someday.

Truth: Someday is not a day of the week.

Solution: Schedule this or admit you're never going to do it and get rid of all those extra picnic supplies, special drink glasses and serving dishes.

Fantasy: You're going to finish that sewing project you started 4 years ago.

Truth: There's something wrong with it, which is why you never finished it. You've forgotten what it is, but have a vague sense of something that wasn't turning out right.

Solution: Take out the item and look it over carefully. Remind yourself of what went wrong so you can learn from your mistakes and then throw it out.

Fantasy: You're going to read all the books on your bookshelves.

Truth: You spend hours in front of the TV and computer. Unless you change your schedule dramatically, you'll never read those books, yet you continue to acquire them.

Solution: Stop buying books and donate most of the ones you have. If you want to start reading more, schedule it. If there's a new book that interests you, check it out from the library.

Fantasy: You're going to start cooking gourmet meals and have bought all the kitchen gear.

Truth: Your counters are covered in unread mail and you go to the drive-through on your way home from work.

Solution: Clean off the counters. Create a menu for a few days of simple dishes you can prepare easily. Grocery shop with a detailed list and schedule cooking your meals at home.

Fantasy: You're going to read that pile of magazines and newspapers in the corner.

Truth: Your life is fine without knowing what's in those publications. You don't have time to do everything in life and you haven't made time to do this.

Solution: Cancel the subscriptions, then put the entire pile in the recycling bin.

Yes, the truth can be brutal and uncomfortable and the solutions may seem extreme. But if you want a new look to your life and home, you have to think and act in a new way.

Be brave and enjoy the results!

The List
September 2010

There's one simple way to transform your life from chaotic and crisis-filled to serene and enjoyable and that's with a pencil and paper. I'm not talking about a 'to-do list" but rather an all-encompassing shopping list, sometimes referred to as a running list. You may already use some version of this list, but I have found that most people would benefit by making it more specific. If you have ever unexpectedly run out of life's necessities, such as computer supplies, band-aids, shampoo, dog food, or a key ingredient in the cupcakes you're making for the school bake sale, then this month's newsletter can help you.

Any time you have to dash to the store for something you need right now, you are in crisis mode. It's a trip you hadn't planned, added to what may already seem like too much to do with too little time to do it. Perhaps the item is something you know you have but can't locate, so running out to the store and buying it again is faster than finding it in your own home. That scenario costs you time and money and can contribute to clutter!

Resolve today to make one change this month and that is to plan ahead and make a detailed list BEFORE you leave your house to shop or run errands. Designate a spot for a shopping list. Keep plenty of pens nearby so it's easy to add to the list. Whenever a family member takes the last one of something such as shampoo, they are responsible for adding it to the list. Until everyone has learned this new habit, take a quick inventory of your cupboards before shopping to be sure that your list is complete. Present this as a useful skill your entire family can practice using. Explain your new system in terms your kids will understand such as "would you like to have a happy parent or a stressed-out crabby parent?" Having (and being able to locate) what you need when you need it greatly reduces the stress of daily life.

If you have adequate supplies but you aren't sure where they are, put your efforts into gathering your belongings and assigning spots for them in your house. Keep similar items together. Involve family members in this process. Children will have definite ideas about where things should live, so do include them. You want your basic everyday supplies to be easy to take out, use, and put away. And everyone needs to agree that putting things back will be part of your "standard of living" so the next person can find the item when they need it.

Before grocery shopping, decide what you are going to eat and check your recipes for the required ingredients. Buy only the amounts you need. Eighty percent of all grocery store purchases are impulse buys, so don't be one of those people trolling the aisles for the latest bargains. It's not a bargain if you buy it and then don't eat it! Just buy what's on your list and leave. You'll save time and money.

If you've ever stood in a store trying to remember exactly which brand, flavor, or version of a product you prefer, making the list before leaving home can solve this dilemma. Be specific and include the brand name, flavor, or any other necessary detail on your list so you buy precisely what you want.

If you use coupons, check them as you are compiling your list. I put an asterisk next to each item on my list for which I have a coupon and I keep the coupons I'm going to use right in my purse with the list.

If your list involves stops at numerous stores, it may be worthwhile to re-write the list to include the store names and any other errands you are running. If I have an especially long list of errands, I'll number them in geographic order so I don't skip any stop. Keep a running list that includes all your errands such as buying a certain light bulb at the hardware store, looking for a picture frame, getting advice at the garden center, trying on a new perfume, taking your boots to the shoe repair, etc. Make one long list or a store-specific list, whatever is easiest for you.

If you are about to enter a store, ask yourself, "What is on my list and what exactly am I looking for?" If you can't answer that question, don't go into the store!

If you think list-making takes too long, I challenge you to time yourself making the list. You'll find that it takes 10 minutes or less. Usually just a few minutes. What is the value of your time and energy?

Creating and using a detailed list is worth the effort.

Stop Interrupting Me!
July 2016

Imagine that you are babysitting a small demanding child who constantly interrupts you. Whether you're sleeping, eating, working, resting, driving, or shopping, moments of activity and peace are frequently interrupted by this child. How long would you put up with that?

Yet, if you own a smart phone or any electronic device, it can be just like that demanding child. Except that in this case you might not be making it stop! Once you recognize the bleeps, bloops, and visual cues as interruptions to the life you're trying to lead, you can choose to tone down the disruptions. Recently, I was setting up a new phone and was appalled to see that the default settings for the apps automatically turned on FOUR types of notifications for each application. I systematically clicked "no notifications" or just a notification in the Notification Folder. If I want to see what's come in, I can just go and check. Until then, I'll be busy living my clutter-free life!

I'm always amazed at how many people I observe taking telephone calls when they're in the grocery store. What is so urgent? Yes, I know sometimes people have to be "on call" for a variety of reasons, but I doubt that applies to most people. Can you give yourself 15 minutes of uninterrupted, concentrated effort on buying food for the heathy meals you claim to want to eat?

This month, I challenge you to turn off your devices and set the Notifications to a minimum. Unsubscribe from all shopping emails or anything else that distracts you. Check your email at intervals, not constantly. Resist the temptation to frequently check Facebook, Pinterest, Twitter, YouTube, News, Politics, etc. When you interact with your devices, tell yourself the truth: How urgent or important was that?

What goals do you have? What's your timeline for those goals? Does being interrupted help or hinder your accomplishing those goals, or is it just a distraction from having to tackle those goals?

Clutter-free living includes consciously choosing to make the best use of your time and energy throughout each day. While modern technology has greatly enhanced our lives, be sure the platforms you choose are worthy of your time and attention.

"People overestimate what they can do in a day and underestimate what they can accomplish in a lifetime."

-Versions of this quote have been attributed to
Bill Gates and Tony Robbins

Improve Your Sleep
October 2016

What's the right amount of sleep for you? Do you get enough sleep?

Inadequate sleep can impair your memory, attention, alertness, concentration, reasoning, problem solving, driving, eye-hand coordination, eyesight, and weaken your immune system. It can contribute to symptoms of depression and age your skin.

Living with clutter has some of the same effects! And clutter in your bedroom multiplies those effects by distracting you from getting a good night's rest. Clutter is like a bunch of stuff that never goes to bed. It whispers or shouts to you "Me! Me! MEEEEEE!!!"

I hereby declare October "Improve Your Sleep Month."

It's been my experience that the larger the Master Bedroom, the more it becomes a repository/hiding place for unfinished projects such as baskets of unmatched socks. Schedule time for the sock-wearers in your family to match and put away their socks. Then create a new habit around laundry so you don't end up with the unmatched sock basket.

Clean out under your bed. Storing things under the bed is terrible Feng Shui, plus the items become magnets for the dirt that accumulates there. Regularly sweep or vacuum under your bed. You'll breathe easier and sleep more soundly.

Turn your mattress. Launder the pillows and blankets. Wash your bedding weekly to minimize dust mites, germs, viruses, and fungus.

Now lie down on your bed. What do you see? Do you see into a messy closet? Don't just close the closet door! Even with the door closed, a messy closet will call out to you in your sleep. Schedule time to clean the closet and practice keeping it clean.

Clear all the clutter from the bedroom floor. If your dresser drawers overflow, schedule time to pare down and donate what you don't love and don't wear.

What's on the bedroom walls? How do they make you feel? Do they need painting, or new artwork? If you were a stranger visiting your house, what impression would you have of the bedroom? Are you giving yourself a nurturing, calming, and loving space in which to sleep? If not, what are you willing to change?

If there's a TV in your bedroom, remove it. If you won't remove it, then cover it at bedtime. The same goes for mirrors. TVs and mirrors can give you the impression that you're being watched.

There's been a lot written recently about the negative effects of using electronic devices right before sleep. Set a technology curfew for the whole family and stick to it!

If you're raising kids or grandchildren, apply the same principles to their rooms. If possible, remove all toys from the bedroom since they encourage interaction and not sleep! I know that lively prints are popular for children's bedding, but if your child has trouble sleeping, try switching to a solid pastel color of bedding and remove all images of action figures or movie characters from the room and see if that helps. Enforce the technology curfew here, too.

Schedule your sleep. Put it on your planner as an appointment with yourself to stay healthy. Don't commit to events that will disrupt your sleep. Do the same for your children. Once in a while is fine; but maintaining regular sleeping hours is the easiest way to establish good sleeping habits.

People with clutter often pretend that they have 25 hours in each day. They over-schedule themselves and then expect others to feel sorry for them because they have so much to do. But the truth is that they've committed to doing too much. If you're sleep-deprived take a good honest look at your schedule. Use this mantra "I'm only one person and I can only do so much." You don't have to do it all, be it all, volunteer for it all, have it all. Part of clutter-free living is giving yourself a realistic schedule, which means that sometimes you will have to say "No" to yourself and to others.

In some circles, it's become a badge of honor to complain about how tired you are. But when you consider the short and long-term serious effects of inadequate rest, prioritizing sleep makes sense. Be a positive role model for others.

Give yourself the time and space to sleep. You'll feel refreshed, energized, and fully alive!

What do you say?
July 2014, Revised September 2016

Do you remember your Mom or Dad replying "What do you say?" in response to your request or demand for something? They were reminding you to say, "please" or "thank you." These are common courtesies that were drilled into us as children. Yet, how often do you use these phrases in daily life?

At the grocery store, I've been noticing how few people say "please" when they order something from the deli, meat, fish, or bakery counter. They may mumble a "thank you" when the food is given to them, but I rarely hear "please." I was tempted recently to say to a woman who had barked her fish order, "And what do you say?" She looked like she might hit me if I did, so I resisted the temptation. What I usually do instead is to say "please" and "thank you" clearly and a little louder than necessary, just to be a good example! It's not an accident that I often get a few extra shrimp or handpicked pieces of fish. Being cheerful and respectful to the person serving me has its benefits.

What does this have to do with clutter? People with clutter can focus too much attention on their personal challenges. Consequently, they don't appreciate what others do for them. How does that food get to the store? All the people who produced it, shipped it, bought it, stocked it, and sold it to you had a role. Recognizing others' contributions to our lives reminds us to be grateful and keeps our attention in the present, away from ruminating on perceived past injustices.

This month I encourage you to say "please" and "thank you" to your friends, your family, coworkers, and to anyone serving you anything or providing a service.

Here are some examples using the word "please" to get you started. I assume you'll be using "thank you" where appropriate, too!

With Family and Friends

• Would you please text me if you're going to be late?
• Please take out the garbage.
• Please help me with my spelling words.
• Can we please schedule a time to discuss this?

With Co-workers

• Please let me know as soon as the client responds.
• Please confirm these dates.
• Please be on time for our meeting.

At the Restaurant

• May I please have some lemon for my tea?
• I'll take the salmon special, please.
• We'll take the check, please.

At the Grocery Store

• May I please have two sourdough rolls?
• I'd like some bacon. Four slices, please.
• I'll take the paper bags, please.

We're all role models for each other in our private lives as well as in public.This month, let's try to make our immediate world a nicer, more respectful place to inhabit.

See how often you can say these "magic words" each day and enjoy the results!

New and Improved
January 2009

The new year is almost a week old. How are your resolutions coming along? This month, I'm suggesting a new way to evaluate all the small choices you make as you navigate your days.

When companies introduce a new product or new packaging, they often call it new and improved. Any change, no matter how small can be labeled "improved." So how can you apply this to your daily life? By recognizing when you are making a choice and asking yourself if that choice will result in an improvement of some sort.

Here's how it works. Your alarm rings in the morning. Before you hit the snooze button, ask yourself if snoozing will improve your life. Maybe, if you need more sleep. Maybe not, if it causes you to be late for work, to feel stressed and rushed, or to skip breakfast. Another way to improve your life might be to set the alarm for 10 minutes earlier and actually get up when it rings! Honestly, if you're rushed in the morning, whose fault is it?

You open the refrigerator to make breakfast and have another opportunity to make choices which improve your life. Just ask yourself, "If I eat this, will it improve my life?" If you take a few minutes to make yourself a healthy lunch, you can avoid asking the improvement question at noon! Before grocery shopping, make a list of the foods that will improve your health and shop from that list.

You are driving to work or taking your kids to school and someone cuts in front of you. Ask, "Will getting upset at a stranger improve my life?" Can you think of a better response to this scenario?

You are at work or at home and you have a task that you don't care to do. Ask, "Will putting off this task improve my life?" Maybe momentarily, but what are the long-term ramifications of procrastination? Another way to reframe the question is "Will taking care of this and doing it right away improve my life?" Visualize the task completed, then get busy and get it done.

You sit down in front of the TV and start flipping through the channels. Ask yourself, "Will watching TV improve my life?" Is there another way to spend your time that would improve your life?

You decide to exercise but are having a hard time committing to it. Ask yourself, "Will exercising right now improve my life?"

Someone wants you to do something that you know you don't want to do. Will it improve your life to say "yes" and be resentful toward that person or do you say "no thanks" and risk upsetting them? Just because someone asks, doesn't mean you are obligated to say "yes." You can even say, "no, not this time, maybe some other time" if that's your honest answer. Learning to set clear boundaries for your interactions with others will improve your life in the long run.

If you have difficulty making decisions, this "improvement question" can help you practice choosing. By making small choices throughout your day, you develop confidence in your ability to choose. You're not aiming for perfection, just an improvement. Focusing on improvement helps you bypass any perfectionist tendencies.

Everything you do every day involves lots of choices. Even if you always do something a certain way, at some point in the past you chose how to do it. As you gain awareness of your choices and assume responsibility for them, it becomes easier to make small improvements by making new choices.

Take ownership of your choices, be honest with yourself, and improve your life!

Tapping Into the Energy of Spring
May 2013

In May we witness the unfolding of Spring in its full glory in Wisconsin. The buds have begun to appear on the branches, the daffodils are blooming and the tulips are poking their heads above ground. Later this month, we'll plant our gardens and flower pots and scan weather reports for final frost warnings.

Use the emerging energy of Spring to re-energize yourself. Spend as much time as you can outdoors, not just working in your yard, but drawing energy from the beauty and wonder of Nature. Then go inside and expend some of that energy decluttering.

If your bedroom is clogged with clutter, start there. A relaxing stroll around your neighborhood after dinner will calm your mind before bedtime. Getting a good night's sleep is one of the best ways to re-energize. The next day, you'll have enough energy to tackle one drawer or the top of your dresser.

Repeat daily until you've cleaned out your entire bedroom and the closet! Inch by inch is a cinch.

Avail yourself of Nature's healing energy.

• Lay on the lawn and look up at the sky and trees.
• Dig in the garden.
• Sit in a chair on your porch or deck and soak up 10 minutes of sun.
• Open your windows and listen to the birds or watch the birds at a feeder.
• Walk around your yard and observe each tiny bud.
• Take a deep sniff from a blooming plant - check for bees first!
• Walk through a greenhouse of flowers and fully experience the riot of colors and textures.
• Roll a bit of lavender or herb leaf between your fingers and breathe in the pungent aroma.

Add a dose of Nature to your daily routine.

• Pack a healthy lunch and eat it outside.

• Take the long way home through the closest city park and drive at the posted speed limit with your car windows open.

• Have an impromptu picnic in your backyard by taking your plate of food and eating it outside.

• The next time you're driving past or near a beach, stop and walk on the beach barefoot.

It only takes a few minutes to plug into the free and priceless energy source of our dear Mother Earth.

The Make Your Bed Challenge

(Invite your family members and friends to join in!)
February 2007

Making your bed every day may not seem like such a big deal. If you don't currently make your bed, you might claim you don't have enough time, or that it doesn't make sense when you just mess up the covers again at night. From my perspective as a Clutter Coach, the simple act of making your bed every day is a small gesture of creating and maintaining order that everyone (age 3 and above) can do for themselves. Committing to making your bed daily is the first step to giving yourself a clutter-free life. It takes less than 2 minutes and is well worth your time and energy. Try it for one month. Invite your family members and friends to join you. Motivate reluctant family members by turning it into a contest!

If you already make your bed, or if you want to step up your commitment to the clutter-free life, try adding one or more of these to your daily list!

- Put away your clothes every day.
- Put away your shoes every day.
- Hang up every clothing item you decide to not wear!
- Fold or roll up your clothing items before putting them in a drawer.
- Close your dresser drawers completely.
- Close your closet doors.
- Make any needed repairs to dresser drawers and closet doors so they function properly.
- When you hang up clothes, button one or two buttons so the garment hangs straight.
- If you drop something, pick it up and put it where it belongs.
- If you see something on the floor that doesn't belong there, pick it up and put it where it belongs.
- When you eat a snack or a meal, clean up after yourself right away.
- When you bring home groceries, put them away immediately. If there isn't room, change your buying habits until you declutter. Only buy what will fit into your available space.

- Keep the inside of your car clean. Throw out trash as needed each time you leave the vehicle.
- Finish tasks ahead of schedule.
- Arrive early for every appointment.

An orderly house creates a calm atmosphere conducive to relaxation and creativity. An orderly life allows lots of time for love, laughter, and joy.

Invest the small amounts of time it takes to maintain order and enjoy the results!

Drop What You're Doing and Go Shop!!

June 2014

What plans do you have for the weekend?

Yard work/gardening?

Golf/softball/bike riding?

Picnic/hike?

Boating/fishing?

Graduation/wedding?

Cook-out/entertaining?

Brewers game/outdoor concert?

Relax/sleep in?

Travel/spend time with family and friends?

In past years, my June newsletter has been about scheduling your summer fun. I'm a big fan of scheduling fun activities. I also believe that if you have something fun to look forward to, it can be a source of motivation to get your work and chores done on time so you can have your fun guilt-free.

That being said, today I want to talk about shopping. Specifically advertisements that implore you to ignore your plans and go shopping.

I understand that businesses need to advertise and that there's a lot of competition for your attention and your dollars. But I really have a problem with the tone of most retail ads. They misrepresent their intentions, they address us as if we're idiots, and they assume we have nothing more important to do than to shop!

Here's what I mean. These are from ad supplements in May, 2014.

"Wake Up Sleepy Head! Super Saturday is Here! Shop Super Saturday Earlybirds 8am-1pm"
First of all, this store has sales ALL the time. Secondly, why should I have to get up early and rush to the store to get these special prices? On this particular Saturday, I was working and unavailable during this crucial sale period.

I just wish stores would have the same prices year-round and let us shop when it's convenient for US!! I know, that's a fantasy, but I can dream, can't I?

Sporting Goods Store - Red, white, and blue ad complete with a waving flag - "Memorial Day Celebration" - Is shopping what Memorial Day is all about?

From the same ad supplement - "Save Today. Vacation Tomorrow." I agree, put money into a travel savings account to save for your vacation. However, this store is not in the business of promoting savings accounts. The rest of the ad copy reads "See how much you could save on RV insurance." Is buying insurance part of the Memorial Day celebration, too?

Home Improvement Store - "Save on the Brands You Trust" - With the exception of paint and mulch, the cover of this ad supplement doesn't mention the brand names of the items pictured.

From the same supplement - "Show Your Lawn Some Love" - was the caption for lawn tools and lawn mowers. So that's why our lawn misbehaves. It feels unloved, poor lawn...

Sports Equipment Store - "Truckload Chair Sale!" What does this mean? Is there a truck full of chairs at every store? Isn't all their merchandise delivered to the store by trucks? Are they too lazy to unload the shipment into the store, so we have to buy them directly from a truck? Based on the prices quoted, you could buy these folding camping or outdoor chairs anywhere and pay the same or less. Also, most of the ad features chairs priced in sets of two. What if I only need one chair?

Department Store - "Black Friday Deals All Weekend! Deals Just as Good as Black Friday All Weekend Long!" Is the second sentence really necessary? How stupid do they think we are?

Nearby it also reads - "Shop Over 170 Door Busters All Weekend During Our Spring Black Friday Sale"

Just in case you think you really overslept and now it's November.

Another Department Store - "Appreciation Sale!" "A Big Thank You Seems Fitting! Styles & Savings Just For You. Plus an Extra 15% Off!"

Sounds personal and inviting, doesn't it, until you realize how many thousands, if not millions of people have received the very same supplement in their newspaper. I don't know why they're thanking me since I never shop there.

The next section of the ad tells a different story. "Prices So Low, You Don't Need a Coupon. Doorbusters In Store Only. Friday 3pm-Close. Saturday 10am-1pm." You can't get these deals online and you have to shop in their store during certain hours. It's like saying, we want your business, but only on our terms. Not so friendly after all.

On Thursdays, do you wander around aimlessly, wondering what you'll do on the weekend? Do you open your email or read the newspaper hoping to find sale flyers? Do you put the special sale hours on your planner so you don't miss out? Probably not! My advice is to ignore these ads.

Whether it's on TV, from a catalog, online, or in a store, only shop when you know precisely what you need and when you will use it. You'll get whatever deal-of-the-day is being offered. The rest of the time, you'll be saving your precious time, energy, and money for the important people and activities in your life.

Have a wonderful summer!

Happy Holidays!
December 2008

Are you dreading the holidays, wondering how you're going to get all the shopping, decorating, baking and other stuff done? If you think holiday preparations include lots of late nights, too much to do with no time to do it, topped off with mounds of January bills, think again.

What is the true meaning of the holidays you celebrate? Whom do you want to be with and what's the most important part of your time spent with others? Will you work yourself to death trying to create your version of the "perfect" holiday or are you willing to consider some alternatives? Here are my suggestions.

Greeting Cards

Excessive: Create homemade cards with handwritten personalized notes, hand-addressed envelopes, special stamps, and decorative stickers.

Send them to everyone you know. Turn these into New Year's cards if you can't quite finish them before the end of December!

Realistic: Send hand-signed cards with computerized address and return address labels. Send them early in December to a reasonable number of people. There are also beautiful cards which can be personalized and sent electronically. You can choose the cards today and schedule them to be sent on the appropriate date.

Skip It: Don't send cards. Try this once and you will discover how many people have been sending cards to you just because they felt obligated to do so! It's a great way to reduce your card list.

Outdoor Decorations

Excessive: String lights on every tree and bush in your yard. Buy extra lights and be sure to include a new decorative item or 2 or 3. Spend lots of time planning the display and shopping for the components. Put up so much stuff that strangers wonder how you pay the electric bill for all the lights! Dread having to take them down in January, or just leave them up until next fall!

Realistic: Use the lights you have and put up what you can in a predetermined length of time. Plug them into a timer set for a few hours each evening. Easily remove them after the holidays.

Skip It: Do not decorate the outside of your house. Take a drive to admire everyone else's lights.

Indoor Decorations

Excessive: Decorate every room in your home including the bathrooms with villages, trees, and other assorted stuff. Shop for new holiday decorations in a special color scheme or theme. Have a train that runs through multiple rooms. Take weeks to install the decorations and months to put it all away after New Year's.

Realistic: Put up one tree, using the ornaments you already own. Create a quality-time tradition by decorating as a family. Allow each child to choose one decoration for his or her room. Only display the decorations you truly love and donate the rest. Have much less stuff to pack away after the holidays.

Skip It: The holidays will still occur even if you don't put up one decoration. If you don't enjoy the decorations or if you just don't have the time/energy this year, skip it!

Baking

Excessive: Bake multiple batches of cookies until you can't stand to see another recipe. Be sure to do all the baking yourself.

Realistic: Bake one batch of cookies and have a cookie exchange with a few friends. Or choose to bake one or two special varieties and teach your kids how to make them.

Skip It: Don't bake at all. Save time, money, and extra calories.

Entertaining

Excessive: Create a themed event which requires shopping for special dinnerware, table linens, and decorations. Agree to attend too many events so you are sleep-deprived and cranky by mid-December.

Realistic: Realize that friends and family are coming to your home to see you, not your special table settings. Use the dishes and table linens you already own. Give your guests your undivided attention.

Skip It: Have another relative host the holiday meal. Say "no" to invitations that don't meet your personal criteria of useful ways to spend your time and energy.

Just because you've always celebrated in a certain way, doesn't mean you have to do it that way.

Choose the holiday activities that are most meaningful to you. Spend quality time with family and friends. Be sure to schedule time for yourself to exercise, sleep, and relax. Let others help you with the "chores."

Happy Clutter-free holidays!

Get Off Your Rear
Go Clutter Clear!
May 2011

This month, I'm challenging you to take action. The time for ANALyzing is over. It's time to do something about your clutter.

Whatever you were taught about the value of belongings may no longer be valid. In today's fast-paced world, some notions about belongings are irrelevant and outdated. The truth is, it doesn't matter who owned or used the item in the past, or what it cost. None of that adds to or subtracts from its true value to you. What matters is whether the possession is useful to you today, right now. Answer these questions:

Do I love it?
Do I use it?
Does it enhance my life in some way?
Does it uplift me?
If it were lost, would I replace it?

If I saw it in a store today, would I buy it?

If you can answer "yes" to at least 2 questions, keep it. If not, let it go. It's as simple as that.

I don't care if you have one messy closet or an entire house filled to the brim. The way to declutter is to begin deciding item-by-item. It's a skill anyone can acquire through regular practice. The more you practice decluttering, the easier and more ingrained it becomes. Start with the easy items and work your way up to the stuff with emotional attachments.

Inch by inch is a cinch. One item today, two tomorrow, three the next day and so on. Not the perfect way, but the get-it-done-now-way. No excuses, rationalization, blaming, or procrastination, just action.

"A journey of a thousand miles begins with a single step." -Confucius

Take action today!

Final Words

Role Model
Dedicated to my Mother
August 2008

In the spring of 2002, I committed to spending every Monday with my mother because I was sure she had only a few left. Instead, the day known as "Mother Monday" continued for over 6 years - at least 317 Mondays in all, but who's counting? On Saturday, July 19, my mother passed away peacefully with me by her side. She was 92. I want to share with you some of her rules for living which she exemplified throughout her life.

Say "Thank You"

When I was in grade school, I attended a birthday party for a girl in our neighborhood. When I arrived home after the party, my mother asked, "Did you say thank you?" I said, "Yes." I knew if I hadn't she would have made me walk the 4 blocks back to the party by myself to thank the birthday girl's mother. A few minutes later the phone rang. It was the mother of the birthday girl expressing her astonishment that I had approached her after the party and thanked her for inviting me. The woman told my mother she had never been thanked like that by a child! She thanked my mother for teaching me good manners and vowed to do the same with her daughter.

My mother always thanked me for the Mondays, for taking her out to lunch, and to her doctor appointments. She also made sure to tell others in my presence how grateful she was to have me as her daughter. As she lay dying, her final words to me, my brother, my husband, and her roommate, were heartfelt, specific "thank yous" to each of us for the roles we had played in her life.

Be Nice

When I was a senior in high school, I received an award. The woman who presented the award gave a short speech which she concluded by saying, "It's nice to be important, but it's more important to be nice." My 18-year-old mind immediately thought,

"No it's not!" But I know now that she was right. In the days after my mother's death, I visited the assisted living facility where she lived for the past 18 months to collect her belongings. I was astounded by the number of people who approached me. Each person told me what a nice lady my mother was and how they personally would miss her. One woman even said, "I'm so glad I hugged her on Friday!"

It wasn't as if she had an easy life, but she approached it with strength and the determination to enjoy every minute of it. Consequently, she brightened the lives of many others. Even when her doctor called me to express her condolences, she mentioned how nice and cheerful my mother had been. The only time my mother disliked someone was if they were mean to her or to others, and then she just tried to avoid contact with them. She understood the value of being pleasant. It never occurred to her to act any other way.

Go while you can.

Everywhere I speak, I ask the question, "If you were told you had 6 months to live, how would you spend that time?" The answers are always the same, travel and spend time with family and friends. After my mother retired, she traveled quite a bit. Any time I told her about plans for an upcoming trip she always said, "Go while you can." I agree!

Live an orderly life.

She didn't say this; she lived it. In our house, Saturday mornings were devoted to cleaning. Everyone had an assignment, my grandfather, my father, my brother, my mother, and I. Cleaning was given the importance and time it deserved and consequently our house was always neat and tidy.

Messes were not tolerated and we were taught to take care of our belongings. When shopping in a clothing store, my mother would go out of her way to hang up clothes that had dropped to the floor. When grocery shopping, she would either take the cart back into the store, or spend some time making sure the carts in the parking lot cart corral were properly stowed. If the aides at the assisted living hadn't collected her newspapers, I would be greeted on Monday with a pile of papers to take away. Order was important to her. She maintained it in her own living space and tried to create it for others wherever she went.

There are people less fortunate who can use what we're not using.

From the time I was old enough to understand, my mother encouraged me to give away the belongings I no longer needed. My father died in 1979. The week after he died, my mother gathered up his clothes and personal items and donated or gave away everything. She missed him the 29 more years that she lived. Getting rid of his possessions didn't negate their relationship.

My mother worked 2 more years before retiring. She stayed in their house until 1990. By that time she had lived there over 40 years. I helped her get ready to sell the house and move into an apartment. Together, it took us only 3 days to go through all of her belongings. We threw out a few old decorations, took several car loads to Goodwill and set aside the furniture she was donating to the women's shelter. Her house sold for full price after a few days on the market. She quickly found a two-bedroom apartment and moved. She lived there 12 years.

In 2002, I helped her prepare to move into a one-bedroom senior apartment. Again, the process took only a few days.

In January 2007, she moved into assisted living. I sold some of her furniture and donated the rest. All she needed was clothing, a lamp, a chair, seasonal decorations and personal items.

She died on a Saturday. The next morning, my brother and I went to her room in the assisted living facility. We threw out the toiletries and packed up her clothes and framed artwork to bring to my house. We encouraged her roommate to take clothing and jewelry that she wanted and would use. We notified the facility that her recliner chair was available to any resident who might need it. That afternoon, I washed her clothes. My brother and I went through the few boxes of her belongings and off-season clothes I had stored at my house. By the end of the day, my car was packed with the donations. On Monday morning we stopped at Goodwill on our way to the funeral home to arrange for her burial. We gave a few more clothes to her roommate and made sure the chair was going to a deserving person. My brother took home a small picture of our parents and I kept two necklaces that I made for her, which I have since donated. She would have been proud of us! We don't need her belongings to honor her memory or to be role models for the lessons she taught us.

My mother proved beyond a shadow of a doubt that you don't need a lot of stuff to live a great life. Her enduring legacy of kindness and gratitude is priceless.

42347520R00116

Made in the USA
San Bernardino, CA
01 December 2016